Repairing and Refinishing Furniture

By J.W. Collier and G.F. Dixon

COLES PUBLISHING COMPANY LIMITED
TORONTO – LONDON – SYDNEY
AUCKLAND – CAPETOWN – SINGAPORE
PRINTED IN CANADA

CONTENTS

INTRODUCTION

There are a number of possible reasons for wanting to preserve old furniture. The most obvious, of course, is that some pieces have a very high market value because of age and authenticity. They may also be beautiful or in some other way visually satisfying. They may simply be typical of their period and therefore museum pieces or collectors' items.

The most important factor, however, is that besides being of attractive shape and good materials, these pieces are often still functionally useful. Comfortable chairs, for instance, were made long before the science of anthropometrics was part of the designer's discipline. Such items may well have a pleasing character as well as being useful and they are therefore worth preserving. But it is possible they will have become damaged during the course of their working life and it is here that the restorer comes in.

The primary aim of this book is to help the amateur who is interested in taking an old and damaged piece of furniture and restoring it to use; preserving its shapes and refurbishing its surfaces. But just as not all old furniture was well made, so not all repairs are well done. Frequently one finds in the shops pieces that have been badly repaired and almost ruined.

We cannot hope to impart the skills of the professional cabinet maker and of the wood finisher in a few thousand words but the instruction given here should make it possible for those with reasonable manual facility to avoid the worst errors and to approach the task with confidence added to enthusiasm.

In the beginning, however, it is wise to have modest aims. Study the fine museum pieces but frequent the secondhand sales as well, purchasing as cheaply as possible the small items that please you and then exercising your growing skills. It can be fun. It can become a fascinating hobby or even a lucrative profession. Not only this but the skills involved will have a much wider application, ranging from original fabrication to a multitude of repair jobs in the home.

We ourselves have been fortunate in combining professional work on modern, reproduction and antique furniture with lecturing and demonstrating at technical colleges. Thus we have experienced the satisfactions of craftsmanship and those of passing on not only skill but enjoyment.

PART ONE

REPAIRING FURNITURE

CHAPTER ONE

ABOUT WOOD

Many of the distinctive features of wood derive partly from the intrinsic nature of the tree and partly from the manner of cutting from the tree to disclose particular features of the structure.

It is not possible here to explore the province of timber technology (which itself includes botanical identification and wood machining) but the following notes may be of some assistance in a rough and ready visual identification.

Oak. Very pale. Pronounced grain pores or pits. Sometimes cut to disclose medullary rays, a series of hard flecks diagonally across the grain. The main furniture wood of Tudor and Jacobean times.

Walnut. Varies in colour from blackish-brown to pale amber with strong veining. Fine but deep grain pits. Many varieties. 'Oyster shell' and 'burr' are special, decorative cuts. Walnut veneers are a feature of the Restoration period through the William and Mary and Queen Anne to early Georgian periods, frequently incorporating marquetry work.

Mahogany. Light, warm brown in colour. Fine but deep cut grain pits. True mahogany responds well to chemical staining but there are many 'mahogany type' substitutes which are less reactive. The most commonly used today is sapele mahogany, a striped variety, in veneer form. Mahogany is the characteristic wood of the great cabinet and chair making of the eighteenth century (Chippendale, Hepplewhite and Sheraton) and of the Regency period.

Tola. Used extensively in some phases of modern furniture. A stripey veneer but darker than sapele, the stripes being closer and a little more diffuse. Tends to darken on exposure.

Rosewood. A rich, exotic timber, characteristically dark, purple-brown veined on a pink background. Frequently tinted red in polishing. Its features show up best under a choice, glossy finish.

Teak. As a veneer it has become the predominant post-war furniture wood. A light, warm brown in colour with fine black veins. Grain cavities fairly pronounced, frequently darkened by resin deposits. Hard and durable. Usually finished with minimum coatings in order to preserve its tactile properies.

Afrormosia. Similar to teak in many of its visual properties and is frequently used in the solid framework of teak articles and for matching chairs. It darkens rapidly.

Beech. A close-textured, hard wood with no grain pits and few surface features. Usually white but may be faintly pink or light brown. Deceptive variations in texture making it suitable to receive water-based stains only. Used for centuries as a basis for ebonising and painting, especially for chairs. Especially suitable, with steaming, for bentwood chairs.

Birch. A close-textured, white wood. Softer than beech. Has few surface features except that a narrow, hard portion resists staining. Often, therefore, used for painting. The Scandinavians, however, frequently employ a semi-pigmented finish. Most frequently encountered as plywood in a variety of grades or as the core material for exotic veneers.

Pine. The main soft wood used in furniture, its special feature being the difference between the dark, hard summer wood and the lighter and softer spring wood. Darkens on exposure to light. Often used in the past as a basis for painting, gilding and veneering. The term 'pine' is often used loosely to cover other coniferous species.

Redwood or Western Red Cedar. Relatively soft but brittle: widely used, nevertheless, for indoor and outdoor cladding because of its stability and resistance to all forms of attack. A light, warm yellow in colour which darkens at first on exposure but subsequently, in clean, exterior conditions, becomes silvery.

Many other timbers have been used in furniture at the dictates of fashion and availability, either for structural or decorative purposes. Satinwood pieces may still be found in sale rooms. Choice occasional furniture in sycamore or 'harewood' (sycamore dyed grey) is still sought after. Makore is much used as a figured mahogany substitute. Elm, ash and chestnut are open-grained timbers sometimes found. Yew, close textured, rather wild, an attractive pale amber in colour, with a multitude of tiny knot markings is once more being used in veneer form. In older furniture ebony and boxwood may be found as banding or in marquetry and inlay work together with dyed fruit woods such as pear. Amboyna, kingwood and mulberry may be encountered in the rare piece. There are many more possibilities that you will discover.

CHAPTER TWO

TO DO OR NOT TO DO

Repairing wooden furniture is a fascinating hobby; maybe this is because no two repairs are ever exactly alike.

Wood as a material is unique. Originally it was a living thing, yet after felling, cutting and seasoning it becomes a workshop material to be used in an almost unlimited number of different ways which are all too easily taken for granted.

From the experience gained in his work, a cabinet maker will will recognise the peculiarities of many different kinds of wood, such as open or close, straight or curly grain, the many and varied textures, the suitability of some timbers against others for a particular type of job, yet he will never find two pieces of wood exactly alike.

It is unlikely that the amateur woodworker will be called upon to repair a rare or genuine antique. Most of the pieces of furniture which come into this class are known, and are either in a museum or form part of a private collection. In the event of any one of these becoming damaged it would be repaired by experts.

When a museum acquires a piece of furniture to add to its collection, the condition of the piece is carefully assessed and any essential repair work carried out by craftsmen employed by the museum authorities before it is put on show.

If an antique dealer buys a damaged piece of furniture he will have a good idea of what the repair will entail and how much it will cost in terms of labour. Once again the work will be carried out by experts and the cost will be recovered when the piece is sold.

What is more likely to happen is that you will acquire a second-hand piece of furniture which, although damaged or broken, could be repaired and made useful again. Either that or an old piece of furniture which forms part of your home will become broken or damaged. It is in these cases that the question arises, 'What is the best thing to do?' If you feel doubtful about your capabilities, then it would be advisable to take expert advice before attempting a repair. Nevertheless, it is generally possible for the average handyman or woman to carry out a satisfactory repair on a piece of furniture, provided that they are given some idea of how to go about it.

The amateur is, generally speaking, handicapped by lack of materials. Finding the correct type of timber, a suitable piece of veneer, or the right fitting always presents something of a problem. Buying a broken piece of furniture, or one which may be of little use in its present form, is perhaps the best way of obtaining materials for this kind of work. The piece should be dismantled carefully, and will no doubt reveal details of the construction used at the time it was made, as well as supplying materials for further use.

Of course modern furniture, as well as old, can be broken and damaged, and the methods used for repair are generally the same, whatever the date of the piece. Provided that you have some knowledge of the type of construction used it is possible to carry out a satisfactory repair, and indeed it is often difficult to get work of this nature done by professionals.

In the following chapters, various types of repairs have been outlined. It may be that the reader will not find the exact answer to his or her particular problem. It should, however, be possible, by following the methods outlined, to carry out all the common repairs.

It is always unwise to take short cuts, and it is for this reason that some details have been repeated. Cleaning off old glue, making and using clamping pieces to protect the work, and allowing glue time to set before going on to the next stage are all essential to a good repair.

CHAPTER THREE

USEFUL TOOLS

It is important that anyone contemplating repair work should have the basis of a cabinet maker's tool kit. The list below indicates those tools which are considered to be essential, and also a number of others which will prove to be helpful.

Boring Tools

Essential

BIT BRACE and DRILL BITS, ¼″ to 1″.

HAND DRILL and BITS, 1⁄16″ to ¼″.

BRADAWL.

Helpful

EXPANSION BIT used in a bit brace to drill holes between 1″ and 3″.

Chisels

Essential

A selection of chisels for general wood work, preferably bevel edged, sizes ⅛″, ¼″, ½″ and 1″.

Helpful

MORTICE CHISELS, sizes ⅛″, ¼″, and 5⁄16″.

Clamps

Essential

'G' CLAMPS, 4″ and 6″.

Gauges

Essential

MARKING for marking width and sizes on lumber before planing or cutting.

Helpful

CUTTING for marking cutting edges on joints, veneered panels before cross-banding, etc.

MORTICE for marking out mortice and tenon, bridle joints, etc.

Hammers

Essential

STANDARD CLAW HAMMER, 10 to 15 oz.

Helpful

MAGNETIC TACK HAMMER for light work with panel pins and tacks.

Knives

Essential

A good all purpose UTILITY KNIFE.

Mallet

Carpenter's pattern.

Oil Stone

India or Carborundum.

Planes

Essential

SMOOTHING PLANE for all general planing.

Helpful

JACK PLANE.

BULL NOSE PLANE.

PLOUGH or ROUTER PLANE with a selection of cutters for all types of grooved work.

REBATE PLANE.

SHOULDER PLANE.

SPOKESHAVE.

Saws

Essential

RIP SAW for cutting along the grain, 26″.

TENON or BACK SAW, 12″.

Helpful

CROSSCUT SAW, 24″.

DOVETAIL SAW for fine cabinet work, 8″ to 10″.

PANEL or VENEER SAW, 20″.

COPING SAW.

PAD or KEYHOLE SAW.

Screwdrivers

8″, 6″, and 4″, SLOT

Sliding Bevel

Square

TRY SQUARE, 6″ and 12″.

In addition to this basic cabinet maker's tool kit, the following list of extra equipment will be found invaluable.

Much will depend, of course, on individual circumstances. If the reader only intends to repair one piece of furniture, then he or she may be able to make do with what tools are available. If, on the other hand, having successfully repaired one or two pieces, he wishes to continue, then extra equipment will most certainly be of assistance and, as will be seen from this list, quite a number of the items are sure to be found in most households.

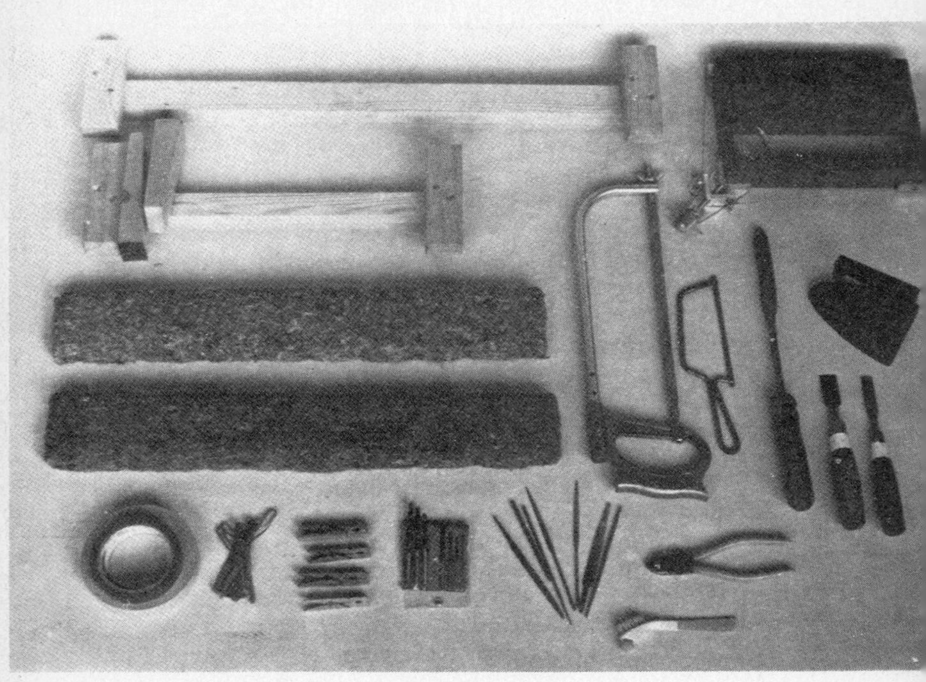

FIGS. 1–15

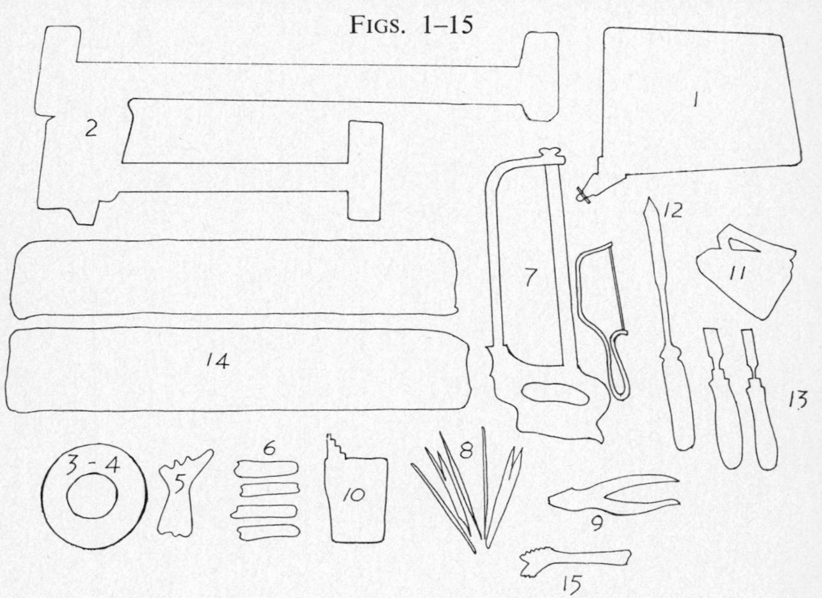

Wire Clamp (Fig. 1). These are generally sold for making picture frames. The size of the clamp can be increased by using a longer wire. This type of clamp can be extremely useful when repairing chair frames, or when several joints have to be glued at the same time. A clothes line or piece of cord used as a tourniquet can also have a similar function.

Wedge Clamp (Fig. 2). This will have to be made and consists of two blocks glued and screwed one on to either end of a strip of wood. Two wedges are used to apply the pressure. Two or three strips of varying lengths will enable work of different sizes to be undertaken.

Masking Tape, Cellotape, Rubber Bands, Clothes Pegs (Figs. 3-6). All of these items will be found very useful for holding small pieces in place while glue is setting, e.g. broken mouldings, pieces of carving or small beads.

Hack Saw (Fig. 7). When dealing with metal work or cutting through timber which contains broken or hidden screws and nails.

Files. (Fig. 8). A selection of files, including some of the small needle type, are very useful when removing or replacing fittings.

Pliers (Fig. 9). A pair of the needle nose variety may be necessary when extracting pins or nails whose heads are flush with a surface.

Drill Bits (Fig. 10). These can be used for a wide range of work particularly when drilling out broken screws or nails.

Flat Iron, Soldering Iron (Figs. 11-12). Either can be used to apply heat to damaged surfaces, bruises, etc. or when dealing with blisters on a veneered surface.

Old Chisels (Fig. 13). Usually short bladed, having been ground down over the years, can be used for chipping out old glue in corners, and removing excess glue when reglueing has taken place.

Fig. 16

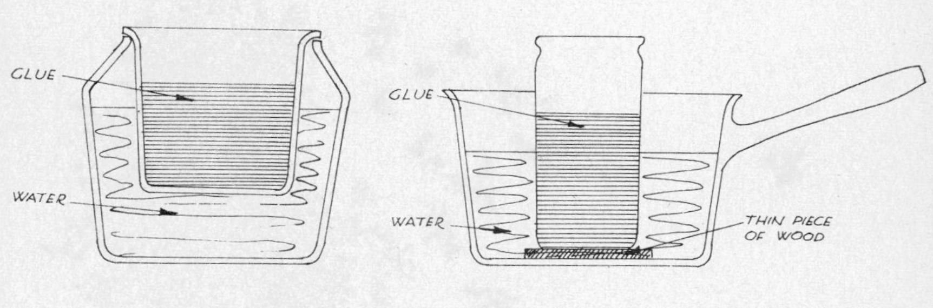
GLUE
WATER
SECTION OF A GLUE KETTLE
GLUE
WATER
THIN PIECE OF WOOD
SECTION OF GLUE HEATING IN A PAN.

Surface Pads (Fig. 14). These, like the wedge clamps, will have to be made, and consist of two pieces of timber (3″ x 1″ of suitable length) covered with thick cloth, underlay or carpet. These are used to stand the piece of furniture on to prevent damage to finished surfaces.

Tooth Brush (Fig. 15). When re-glueing an old break, the edges will all be dirty, and unless the surfaces are cleaned, fresh glue will not stick. An old tooth or nail brush used dry will often enable these surfaces and corners to be cleaned.

CHAPTER FOUR

ADHESIVES

For a great many years Scotch glue or animal glue has been the traditional adhesive used by the cabinet maker. In the 1930's resin traditional adhesive used by the cabinet maker. In the nineteen-thirties resin adhesives were introduced and developed rapidly for wartime use, and now they have superseded animal glue for furniture construction.

Scotch glue still has its place, and is in fact the only glue that can be used for hand veneering. The amateur may well find some of the modern adhesives more convenient for general glueing, and that he need only use animal glue when dealing with veneered work. For all the repairs described in the following chapters it is assumed that resin adhesive will be used unless otherwise stated.

Animal Glue. It is possible to buy animal glue in either slab, pearl or powder form. Whichever type is used, the mixing is similar. (Slab glue must be broken into small pieces and to do this it is advisable to wrap the slab in a piece of hessian or similar material to prevent the pieces from flying about and endangering the eyes. A normal medium weight hammer will be the most suitable tool to use for this.) It is essential when dealing with this glue that a two-part pot be used. The traditional glue kettle is best and they are still obtainable (Fig. 16). Failing this, the glue may be put into a can which is then placed in a pan of water. The tin must not be allowed to rest on the bottom of the pan. Place the glue in the container and just cover with water. After an overnight soak the contents will have taken the texture and appearance of a jelly and are now ready for heating. Glue should never be allowed to boil, and it is ready for use when it attains the consistency of cream.

Each time glue is re-heated it loses some of its strength. When using this type of glue it is important that the parts to be glued are warmed prior to application, otherwise it will chill. It is therefore necessary to work quickly and clamps should be pre-set during a dry assembly, with clamping pieces between the clamp and the work to prevent damage, and also to ensure that the pressure applied by the clamps is spread evenly over the full area. Everything must be ready to hand before the actual glueing is started. Excess glue may be removed with a damp cloth when the joint is made, or with an old chisel when the glue has almost set. If the surrounding surfaces have been polished, the glue will not stick and any excess may be carefully chipped off with a chisel after the glue has fully set. The clamps should be left on for several hours, preferably overnight, to allow the glue to set completely.

Resin Glues. These have been developed in various forms and may be obtained from most hardware and hobby stores. They are usually available in two-part packs, which when mixed are used cold, and when set they are also waterproof. Once set they cannot be re-activated. Although used cold the setting time can be shortened by the application of heat. The manufacturer's instructions for mixing, which must be followed carefully, will also give details of setting times at different temperatures.

With all these glues it is important to follow the manufacturer's instructions. If you do not follow the instructions it is useless to complain that the glue is no good.

Contact Cement. These adhesives are useful in repair work where clamping may not be possible. Originally developed for fixing decorative laminates, they do give a good wood-to-wood bond. Each surface should be given a thin layer of glue, which must then be allowed to stand until it is touch dry. The pieces must be brought together exactly in the required position, as no movement is possible once they have made contact.

All Purpose Bondfast Glues. These glues are easy to use and very effective when used correctly, i.e. allowing a proper drying time. Most companys make one. **All Purpose Bondfast,** is milk white in colour and usually come in a plastic container, either a squeeze bottle or a larger jug.

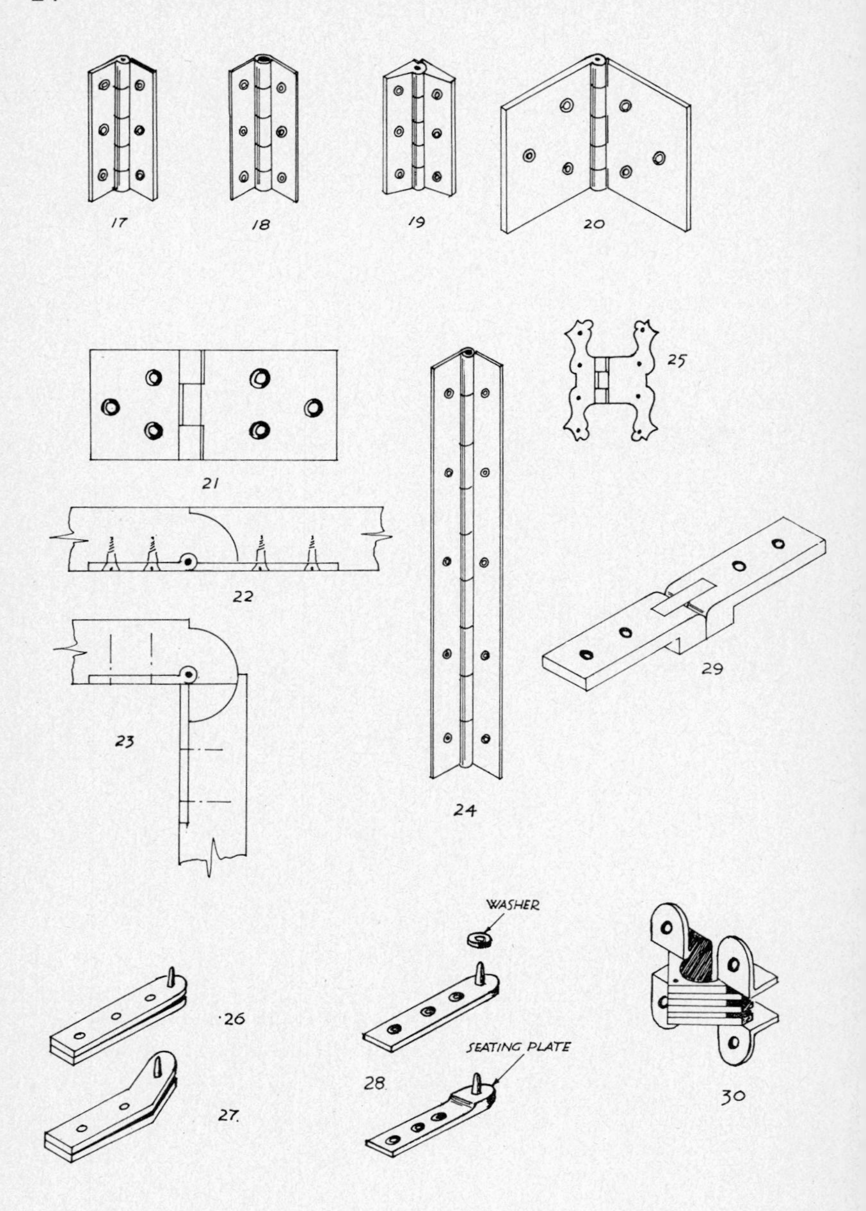
17
18
19
20
21
22
23
24
25
29
WASHER
26
27
28
SEATING PLATE
30

CHAPTER FIVE

HARDWARE

Most of the moving parts in furniture, apart from drawers, are linked together by metal fittings, often made of brass. Hinges are the most common fitting in general use and many types have been designed to cover a wide variety of needs. The following are examples of some you can expect to find on old furniture.

Butt Hinge. Cabinet doors. Fig. 17 solid drawn brass butt. Fig. 18 a cheaper variety constructed from thinner sheet brass and bent round the pin.

Stopped Butt (Fig. 19). Casket or box lids. Opens only to 90°.

Back Flap (Fig. 20). Bureau fall flaps. Note wide plates. Provides a level surface when flap is open.

Rule Joint (Fig. 21). Fall leaf on gate-leg tables. Countersunk on opposite side to knuckle, with one flap wider than the other to allow for the hollow in the flap edge. Fig. 22, flap in up position; Fig. 23, flap down.

Piano Hinge (Fig. 24). Piano lids and sometimes cabinet doors. Produced in lengths between 2′ and 6′.

Butterfly Hinge (Fig. 25). Decorative hinge for cabinet doors. Fitted to outside face of door and carcase framework.

Pivot (or Centre Hinge) (Figs. 26-28). Often used on glazed cabinet doors where if a butt were used one door would swing out and prevent a second one from opening. Fig. 26, straight; Fig. 27 necked.

Card Table (Fig. 29). For folding tops, allowing the leaf to turn through 180°.

Soss (Fig. 30). Cabinet doors where the hinges will not be seen when the door is closed.

Some of the faults which develop in these moving parts can be traced either to wear in the fitting or, more often, movement of the timber, such as shrinkage, warping or swelling. When faced with the problem of a sticking door, or one that will not shut properly, inspect it carefully to ascertain the cause. It could be due to movement in the door, the carcase or the hinges. Continued use of such a door may have caused the hinge to work loose, the screws having been pulled. The easiest way to refix the hinge would be to use longer screws of the same diameter, but this you can only do if the thickness of the timber will allow.

If longer screws cannot be used, then the holes must be plugged. This is done by cutting small pieces of wood, tapered to fit the old screw holes, glueing and tapping them home. When the glue has set the tops of the plugs should be trimmed flush with a sharp chisel. New screw holes can be started with a bradawl. When replacing screws after plugging, or inserting them into a replacement piece of timber, a steel screw of the right size should always be used for the first time. Brass screws can so easily be broken off, and one is left with a drilling job. It is also helpful when refitting hinges to put only one or two screws in place until the work is completed. This will allow for any adjustment should it become necessary.

If the sticking of the door is due to *swelling*, the door should be removed and allowed to stand in a dry atmosphere. The drying process can be helped if the binding edge, which will be marked by continual rubbing, has either a shaving taken off or is rubbed down with sand-paper, thus allowing any moisture to escape.

Sometimes a door will not close properly because the screws in the hinges are too big. This may have occurred over a period of time, the original screws having been worked loose for some reason and then replaced by bigger ones. The choice here is either to countersink the hinge itself, thus allowing the screw head to bed correctly, or to re-plug the holes and put in screws of the correct size.

It may be that after repairing a split in the end of a cabinet (see page 32) it is now narrower than the top and bottom, so that they stand proud, thus preventing the door closing. It will be necessary to plane these in order to get the surfaces level once more.

Wear in a butt hinge is not a comman fault, but it can happen when pivot hinges are being used. The seating plate or the washer on the bottom hinge may have become worn, and it will be necessary either to replace the washer or to fit a new hinge (see Fig. 28). If a new hinge is required it would be advisable to remove the old one and take it with you when you are purchasing a replacement.

The **rule joint** used on some gate-leg tables is very reliable, but can occasionally give trouble, and this is more often than not caused by swelling of the timber. The diagram in Fig. 22 shows a section of the joint and it will be seen that the leaf and the top are held at a fixed distance apart by the hinge, so that any swelling in the timber must cause them to rub against each other. The treatment is much the same as that described for a sticking door, i.e. remove the flap and allow to stand in a dry atmosphere. It will assist the drying out process if the shaped surfaces are sandpapered to remove any polish, again to allow moisture to escape.

Another group of fittings are those concerned with holding moving pieces in a fixed position, namely locks, stays and catches. The following list describes the various types and where they are used.

Straight Cupboard Lock (Fig. 31). Screwed onto the inside surface of a door. The bolt shoots through from side to side so that the lock may be used for either left or right hand opening.

Cut Cupboard Lock (Fig. 32). The framework of the lock is let into the inside and edge surfaces of the door. These are made for either left or right hand fitting.

Till or Drawer Lock (Fig. 33). The framework is let into the inside and top edge of the drawer front. The bolt, when out, enters a mortice cut into the underside of the top rail, which is sometimes fitted with a striking plate.

Box Lock (Fig. 34). The framework is let into the inside and edge surfaces of the box or casket, and also has its own special locking plate set into the edge of the lid, allowing the two bolts to move up and sideways when locked.

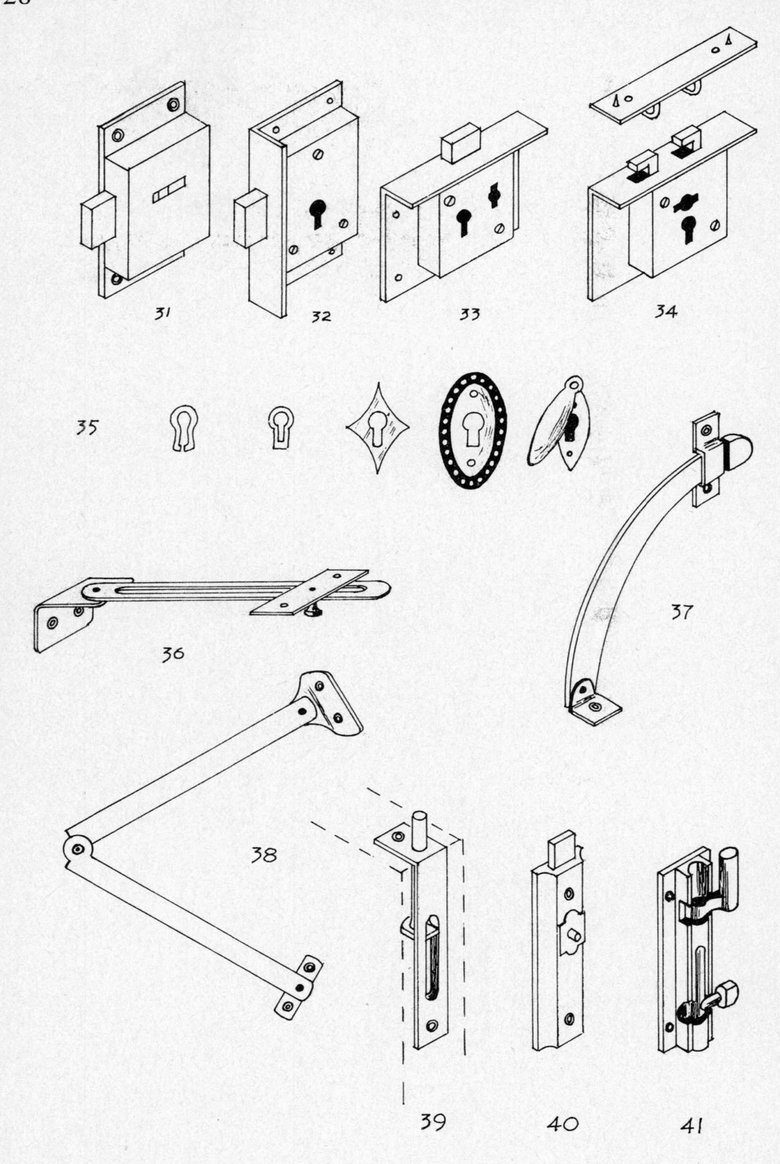
31
32
33
34
35
36
37
38
39
40
41

Escutcheons (Fig. 35). Decorative keyholes which also fill a practical need, as they tend to protect the surface around the keyhole. May be made in brass, ivory, boxwood or other hard decorative materials.

Wardrobe stay (Fig. 36). Fitted to heavy wardrobe doors to prevent them from swinging open too far.

Quadrant stay (Fig. 37). Fitted to flaps and fall fronts and may be for left or right hand fitting.

Rule-joint stay (Fig. 38). Fitted to flaps and lids and are available for either left or right hand fitting.

Flush Bolt (Fig. 39). Usually cut into the back or edge surface of one of a pair of doors. Bolt shutting into a hole drilled into rail or carcase framework.

Cupboard Bolt. Screwed onto the inside surface of the door. May have either a straight bolt (Fig. 40) or cranked bolt (Fig. 41). The stop is provided either by a small metal angle bracket or by a hole in the carcase framework.

Faults in this group of fitting may also be due to the movement of timber, or to fixing screws having worked loose, in which case the repair treatment will be the same as that described for hinges. With locks, the failure may be due to a broken spring or damage to the carcase or rails around the hole.

Locks should be carefully removed, trying not to damage screw heads or the surface of the lock itself. If the framework of the lock is screwed then it will be easy to remove the cover to reveal the working parts. If it is riveted, then they should be punched lightly and the cover gently pried off. Broken springs can generally be replaced at a good locksmith shop, and it is worth the effort to obtain a new spring so that the original lock can be used again in preference to fitting a new lock. Make sure when replacing the screws that they are holding properly. If in doubt the holes should be plugged, as described on page 26.

Breakages around a bolt or lock mortice can sometimes be repaired by re-glueing if the piece is still available, but generally it is better to cut out around the damaged part and fit in and glue a new piece which should be of the same kind of timber, or a similar type which can be stained and polished to match the original finish. The method for fitting a new piece is carried out in a similar manner to that described on page 41 for a worn drawer rail, except that if the damage is round a lock mortice in the middle of a drawer rail, it should be bevelled at each end.

It is sometimes difficult to mark the exact position for a hole or mortice for a lock. The best way to do this is to smear the end of the bolt with the sediment usually found on the end of an oil stone block. The bolt or lock should be worked in and out several times with the door or drawer in the closed position, and when it is opened it will be seen that the required position has been marked quite clearly.

CHAPTER SIX

GENERAL REPAIRS

Cabinets—Tables—

Surface Damage and Chairs

The basic part of any cabinet, sideboard, wardrobe, cupboard or bookcase, is a carcase or box. This forms the main structure of the piece. When faced with the problem of carcase repairs, one should not take apart more than is absolutely necessary. The work will generally fall into one of three groups, (*a*) joints which have become loose, (*b*) the repair and replacement of damaged or missing parts, and (*c*) the repair of worn parts.

When the fault is a **loose joint,** take a good look at the construction, and see how the various component parts are fitted together. It may be necessary to remove one or more pieces which are attached to the part forming the joint you are going to re-glue. Having made sure that the joint is now free, carefully knock the pieces apart, always using a piece of scrap timber (2″ x 1″ or similar) to ensure an even pressure and to prevent splitting from the blows with either a hammer or mallet. Any old glue left on the inside surfaces of the joint must be cleaned out, and this can probably best be done using an old chisel.

For re-glueing the joint, clamps are usually needed, and they should always be pre-set, with suitable clamping pieces, and the glueing carried out as described in the chapter on Adhesives.

When dealing with **broken parts,** the same preliminary inspection should be carried out. A split end may require the removal of the end itself, but it would be quite unnecessary to dismantle any further. Care must be taken to support the remainder of the carcase otherwise more joints may become strained. Splits are usually due to shrinkage.

If the split is along the line of a joint which has opened (Fig. 42) then it is essential to plane both surfaces flat and level, taking off as fine a shaving as possible, as this will make the end fractionally

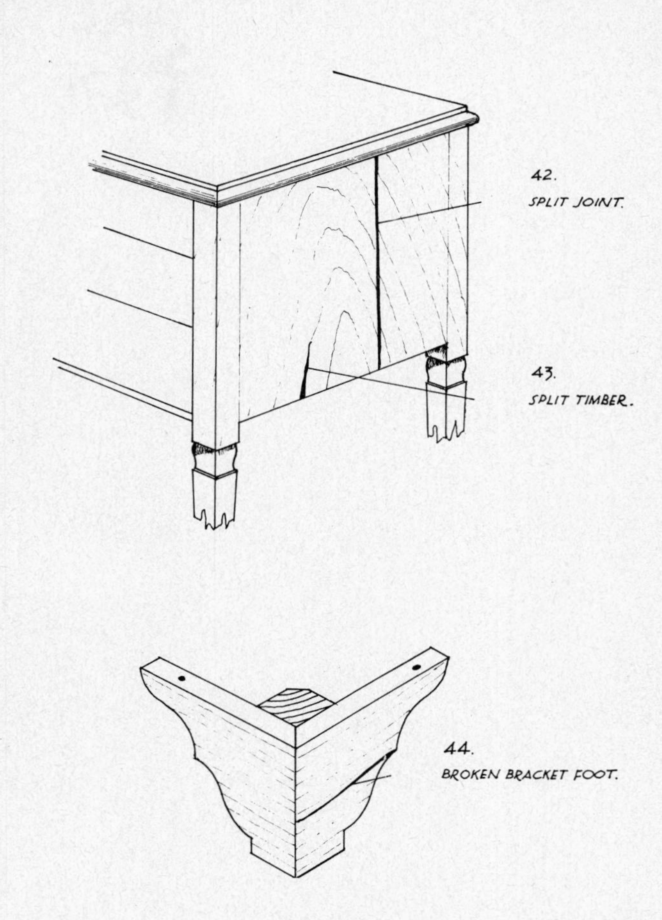
42.
SPLIT JOINT.
43.
SPLIT TIMBER.
44.
BROKEN BRACKET FOOT.

narrower. When re-glueing, clamps will have to be used, and care must be taken to see that the ends of both pieces are flush, and also that the surfaces are flat and level.

A split in the timber itself may only run a few inches (Fig. 43) and will follow the grain, tapering away to its end. In such a case it is possible that the repair can be carried out without removing the end itself, and, if the carcase joints are sound, it would be foolish to do so. The thin end of the split will need to be widened, and this can be done by working into it with the tip of a dovetail saw blade. A ‘feather wedge’ is then cut from a suitable piece of timber or even a thick or ‘sawn cut’ piece of veneer. The piece will need to be tapered along its length and also across its width, to ensure a tight fit when it is pushed into the split after glueing. Leave until the glue is hard then trim down carefully without damaging the surface. Always check that the surfaces are still level. This can be done either with a straight edge or with the blade of a square, on the opposite side to that being wedged.

When dealing with a broken piece, e.g. the **bracket foot** (Fig. 44), the type of repair will depend on individual circumstances.

If the break is a new one, and this is the best time to effect a repair of this nature, the broken edges will be clean and sharp. It is often possible to glue the two pieces together again, using only a very thin application of glue, holding in place with masking tape or cellotape until the glue has set. Any excess glue should be carefully cleaned off before taping. It is also essential to support the piece of furniture, so that the damaged foot is not under pressure.

If the break is an old one, the edges will be dirty and possibly burred over, so that the glue will not stick properly unless they are cleaned. This can be done by using an old dry toothbrush, care being taken not to break off any splinters which may be left. When cleaned in this way the two parts should be put together to see if a reasonable joint can be made. If this is possible, and the break line is not too obvious, then the joint may be glued and taped in the same way as a new break. When a good joint cannot be achieved, then a new part will have to be made, using the broken pieces as a pattern to get the required shape. If it is possible to obtain a piece of timber of the same kind, so much the better, if not, try to use a piece with similar grain and texture which can be stained and polished to match the original finish.

Care must be taken when dismantling the foot. If the fixed part is held by a glued joint, heat applied by a warm iron on a wet cloth will help to soften the glue and enable the joint to be taken apart. Do not use an excess of water with this method as it could easily cause the timber to swell. When the new part has been made and fitted it should be glued, and in this case clamps will be needed to hold it in place. It is often necessary to make shaped clamping pieces to prevent a surface becoming marked or damaged, and also to allow for an even and square pull by the clamps.

It may sometimes happen that part of the broken piece is missing, and, in the case of the bracket foot, replacement will be the same as that just described, except that a pattern will have to be made from the opposite foot. This can be done by cutting a piece of cardboard to the required shape. When a shaped part is completely missing, with no other piece forming a 'pair' to obtain a pattern, the only solution is to visit museums or a library, looking for a similar piece of furniture or an illustration from which it may be possible to make a drawing of the missing part in order that a pattern can be made.

Old dried glue which may be in the joints left open by the loss of the part must be cleaned out, again using an old chisel, and new joints cut to fit. Once this has been accomplished, the new piece should be cut to shape, cleaned up and glued in place. The original part may have been held by screws and/or glue as well as the end joints. An old glue line or old screw holes will tell you, and the new part should be fitted in the same way.

Cocked Beads are a small decorative feature often found around the edges of doors and drawers on eighteenth-century furniture, and they are easily broken off and sometimes lost. They can be fitted in a variety of ways. On doors they often take up the full thickness of the door, on drawers one may find that the top and bottom beads are full thickness, with the side beads fitted into a rebate, which still allows the dovetails to show (Fig. 45).

If the break is a new one and the piece is still available, then it can be glued, put into place and held by a clamp until the glue has set. Take care to use clamping pieces to avoid any damage to the surfaces. If the piece is missing there are two alternatives depending upon individual circumstances: (*a*) the broken part can be trimmed off, by cutting across the bead with a sloping cut (Fig. 46) and a new

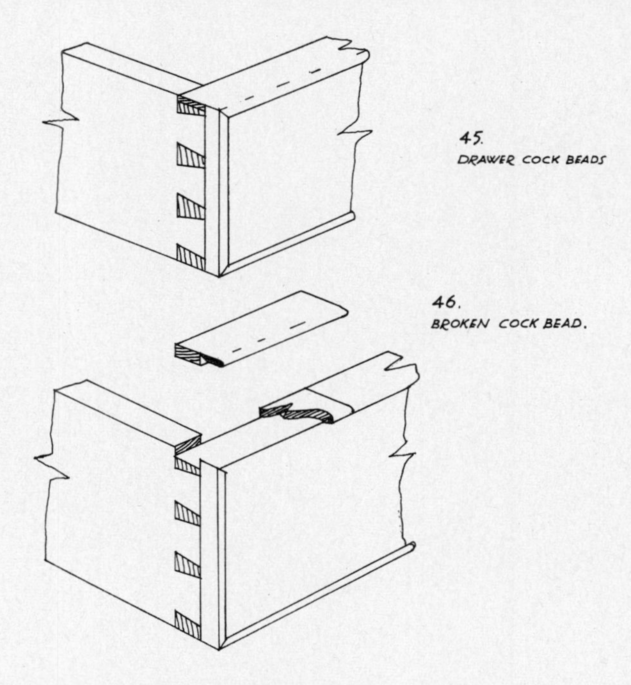

45.
DRAWER COCK BEADS

46.
BROKEN COCK BEAD.

piece made with its end bevelled to fit the angle of the saw cut; (*b*) the remaining part of the bead can be removed entirely and a new one made to replace it. Any old glue must be cleaned off the surface before the new bead is fitted. In either case the timber used should be of the same kind as the original or as near to it as possible. When the repair is on a drawer front, special attention should be paid to the end joints if the top or bottom bead is being replaced as it will show a mitre at the front, but will overlap the actual joint at the back. The rounded edge should be sandpapered to a finished surface, using a cork or wooden sanding block, before the new bead is glued on. This will prevent the finished front surfaces of the drawer or door becoming damaged.

The **mouldings** in a glazed door sometimes need repair or replacement. Details of the construction are shown in Fig. 47. In the case of a shaped or rounded topped door the outer edges of the glass may be held in place by putty. If the edges are straight, then the whole door may be beaded.

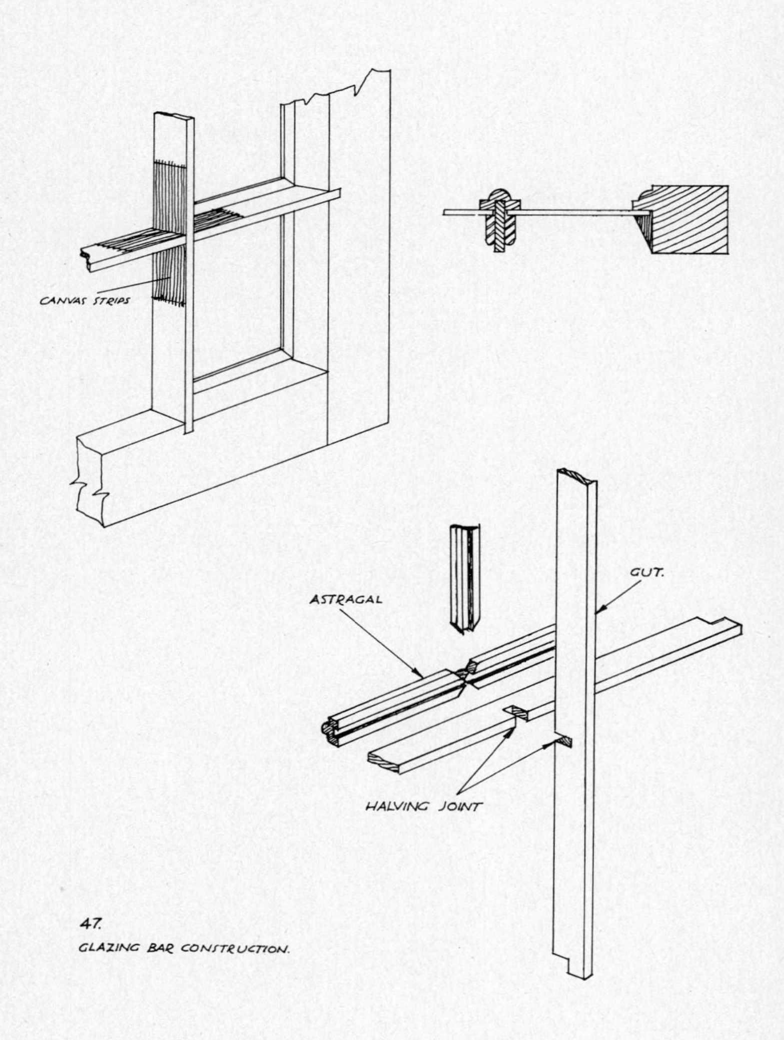

47.
GLAZING BAR CONSTRUCTION.

In either case the glass must be removed before commencing repair work. Any damaged or loose joints in the actual framework of the door must be made good before attempting any work on the glazing bars. Follow the methods described for carcase work and do not take apart more than is necessary, otherwise the whole door will have to be rebuilt. Any damage to the ribs, or guts as they are sometimes called, should now be repaired or replaced. The joints are usually a simple halving. After glueing, these joints can be strengthened either by glueing across the corner a small strip of thin canvas or by putting in a strip of masking tape. The moulded section fits onto the top of this framework, and it may be possible to buy a length of moulding, but if not, new pieces can be made using a plough and/or rebate plane to get the main section, the rounded part being worked with a bull-nose plane prior to sanding to a finished surface.

Care must be taken when cutting the end joints, and they should be cut with a sharp chisel. If you look at the remaining original joints, it will be seen that they always bisect the angles of the joining mouldings.

Mouldings that are worked on tops and edges, or used as a decoration (other than cock-beads) applied to drawer fronts and doors, often become damaged or have pieces missing. This usually happens because they overhang or stand proud of the main surfaces and are more easily knocked.

In the case of the moulding which has been worked around the edges of a table top, the damage will most likely be at a corner which has been knocked and the timber crushed. The damaged area must be cut off and a new flat and level surface planed across the corner (Fig. 48). A replacement piece of timber of the same kind is cut wider and thicker than required. This must have one edge planed flat and level to provide the surfaces for a rubbed joint. Bondfast glue is the most suitable for this type of repair. When brought together

they are rubbed gently but firmly along the length until adhesion is felt. The pieces are then left to set overnight. When set, the replacement piece is planed down to the required thickness and its edges cut to follow the original outline of the top. The shape of the actual mould can now be worked along the edge, care being taken at all

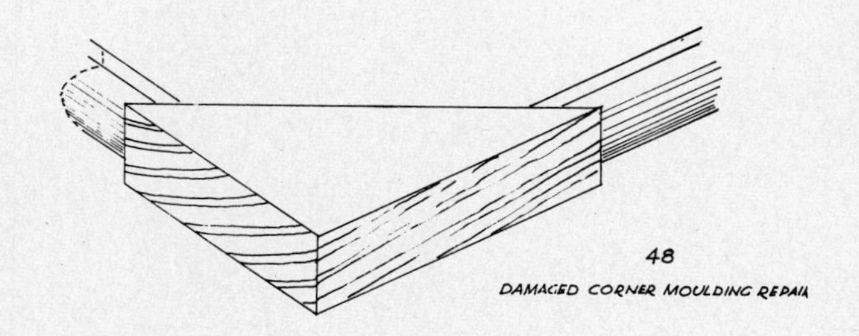

48

DAMAGED CORNER MOULDING REPAIR

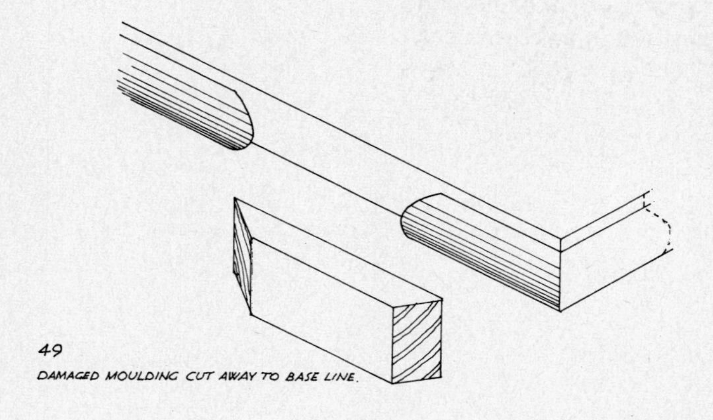

49

DAMAGED MOULDING CUT AWAY TO BASE LINE.

times to avoid marking the original surface. Sandpaper held round a block, or cork rubber made to fit the shape of the mould, can now be used to complete the job.

When the damaged part is in the length of the moulding, and not at a corner, two angled cuts outside the damaged area are made and the crushed part chiselled out to provide a flat surface on the inside or base line of the mould (Fig. 49). A new piece is cut with its ends angled exactly to correspond with the part removed, and then glued into place. When set, the shaping and finishing is carried out in the same way as that described for a damaged corner.

The type of moulding used as a decorative feature for drawer fronts and doors of Jacobean and similarly styled pieces are known as *applied mouldings;* that is to say they are glued onto the surface. Damage in this case usually means that a piece of moulding has come off. If the piece is still available it is important that all the old glue is cleaned off the surfaces before an attempt is made to re-glue. Clamping may be necessary and care must be taken to protect the mould from damage while this is being done. If the piece is missing it may be possible to obtain a length of moulding of the same section from a hardware store or a lumber yard. The new piece should be cut to size, and it will usually be found that the ends are mitred to fit into the pattern of the original moulding (Fig. 50). Once again all old glue must be cleaned off prior to the new piece being glued into place. The section of the new moulding should be sandpapered before glueing.

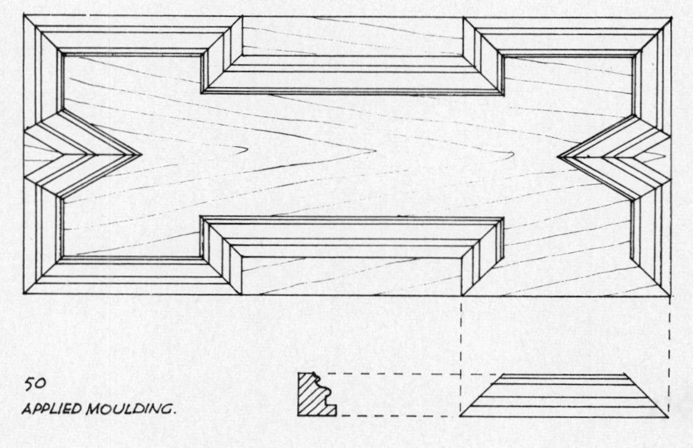

50
APPLIED MOULDING.

General wear and tear is often associated with moving parts, especially **drawers.** Worn drawers usually suffer from loose joints, worn under-edges of sides, broken bottoms and worn drawer runners.

If the main joints of a drawer have become loose, then it should be carefully dismantled. Start by removing the bottom, which may be held at the back by screws or nails, and also by small glue blocks along the underside edge of the drawer front. These will have to be chipped off with a sharp chisel and new ones made to replace them. It will now be possible to tap out the sides from the front and back. If one or more of the joints should remain firm, then it must be carefully knocked out with a hammer, using a scrap piece of timber to spread the blow and prevent the sides from splitting. Any old dried glue must be removed from all dovetails, taking care not to chip out any wood as this will spoil the joint when re-glued. If the only defect is loose joints, then they may simply be re-glued and put back together again. Clamps may be necessary depending on how loose the joints had been. Clamping pieces should be used and a piece of newspaper placed between them and the glued joints to prevent them from sticking. Check the drawer for squareness across the diagonals, carefully clean out any excess glue which may show on the inside corners, and replace the bottom. If glue blocks had been used originally, they should now be replaced.

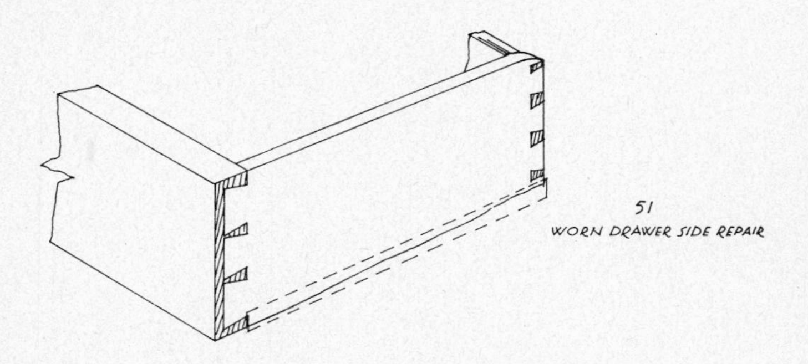
51
WORN DRAWER SIDE REPAIR

When a drawer does not run smoothly, or jerks when opened or closed, it is generally a sign that the sides are worn. A look at the bottom edge of the sides will verify this, and usually it will be seen that they are worn away (Fig. 51) with the greatest wear being towards the back. It will be necessary to cut away and replace the worn parts. To do this, cut the side down parallel with its top edge, taking off just enough to clear the worn part. It will not be possible to use a smoothing plane to do this as the drawer front will project below the required line. The best way will be to cut down to the line with a sharp chisel, working with the sharpening bevel downwards to prevent it digging in and splitting the side. It is generally possible to finish off with a bull-nose plane, to get a smooth flat surface. Cut a suitable piece of timber slightly oversize and plane one edge flat and level to give a good joint with the new edge of the drawer side. Glue and clamp into place. When the glue has set, plane the new piece to the required size, taking care not to damage the original surface of the drawer side, and then refit the drawer. A rub with wax along the bottom edge will often help a drawer to run smoothly.

Generally when drawer sides show this kind of wear, the runners will also need attention. In this case the damage will be towards the front and will also include the front rail (Fig. 52). The runners can be replaced fairly easily as they are usually held by a screw at the back, and are stub-tenoned into a groove in the back of the front rail. Sometimes they may be glued near the front, but after removing the screw it will be fairly easy to free them with the aid of a chisel pushed between the back end of the runner and the carcase side. The worn part of the rail will have to be cut out, and this is done by

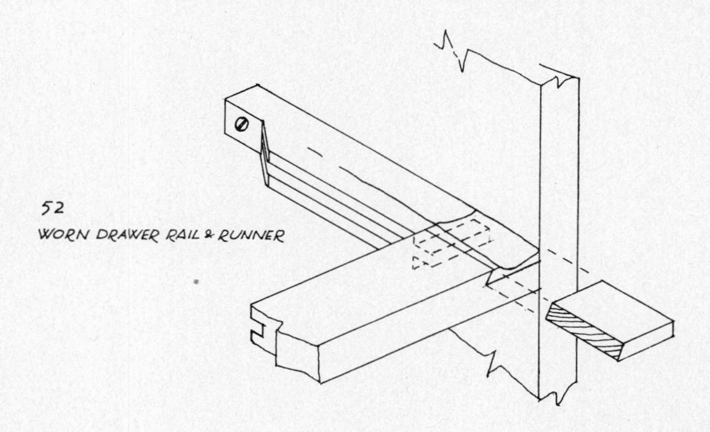

52
WORN DRAWER RAIL & RUNNER

sawing across it down to the depth of the wear, cutting at an angle, which will help to hold the new piece in position. The damaged part should now be cut out carefully with a sharp chisel, leaving a bottom surface that is flat and level. The new piece should be of the same kind of timber as the rail, and cut oversize in width and thickness, so that its surfaces can be levelled after glueing, and its edge bevelled to fit into the angle of the cut made into the rail. When glued, the piece is gently tapped into place and held with a 'G' clamp until set. After the surfaces have been levelled off and sandpapered, the new runners can be fitted, and these should be of a suitable hardwood. It is advisable to glue the tenon and a little way up the side. The back will be held by the screw, which should have a slotted hole to allow for any movement in the carcase timber.

Returning to the drawer itself, one more possibility of damage is that the bottom may have split. This will be the case when the bottom is made from solid timber which may have been jointed to make up the required size. The bottom must be removed, and this will mean taking out any screws or nails which hold it at the back, and also glue blocks at the front if they have been used. (In a well-made drawer, the screws holding the bottom will be in slots, not holes, to allow for shrinkage.) The edges which have come apart will need to be planed flat and level before they are re-glued. Sometimes drawer bottoms are made with a little extra width sticking out beyond the back to allow for shrinkage, and if this is the case the bottom may still be big enough even when the joint has been replaned. If not, then the back edge must be planed flat and level and a new piece prepared and glued on to make up the required width.

When re-glueing the original split, and the extra piece if required, clamps will almost certainly be needed and the main problem will be to keep the bottom flat. Use some form of weight (such as a full bucket of water) applied on the top to make sure the surface stays flat when pressure is applied by the clamps.

Before replacing the bottom, check the screw holes. Whether the original ones are to be used again, or new ones have been made in an added strip, they should be slotted to allow for shrinkage (see Fig. 53).

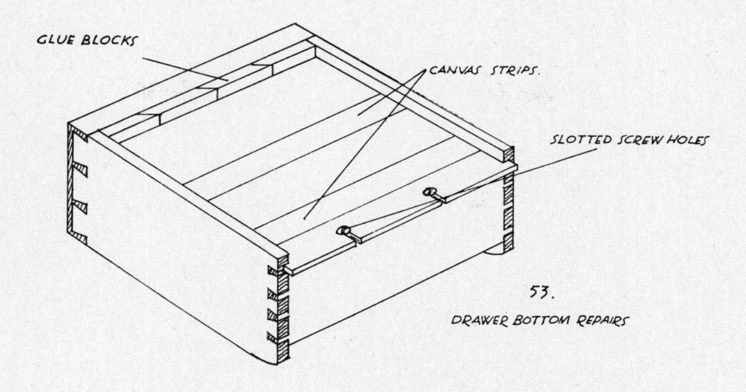

53.
DRAWER BOTTOM REPAIRS

The **draw-leaf table** is possibly the most popular form of extending dining table, and the construction used today is basically the same as it ever was. The leaves are drawn out and raised to the level of the centre top by means of tapered bearers running on guides and through slots cut into the main framework of the table. After a considerable amount of wear the leaves may tend to droop when opened and this is caused either by wear on the bottom surface of the slots or by wear on the bearers themselves. If it is the slots that are worn, small pieces of wood should be cut to size and placed on the under surfaces, thus increasing the amount of lift. The level of the top with the leaves extended should be checked, and if it is satisfactory the pieces of wood should be glued into place. In the case of worn bearers the best solution is to replace them completely and a hardwood such as beech ought to be used for this. The old bearers may be used as a pattern, but a check must be made first to ensure that they are not bent or warped.

A second form of extending table, dating almost as far back as the draw-leaf, is the **gate-leg table.** Wear and tear on the moving parts of the tops on this type is dealt with on page 27, under the heading **rule-joint.** The gate itself may function by a metal hinge or, on the better quality and older tables, by means of a **knuckle joint.** This type of joint (see Fig. 54), will stand up to a remarkable amount of wear, but over the years it can of course work loose. If the wear is not excessive a simple repair can often be made by knocking out the centre pin and then, with the gate clamped to the main framework

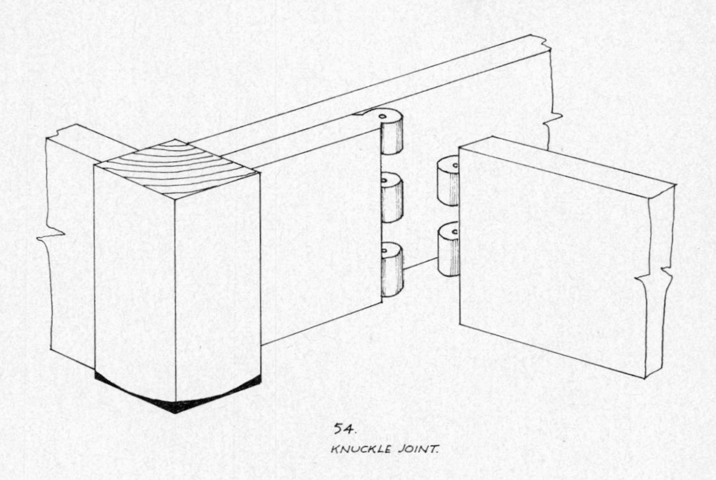

54.
KNUCKLE JOINT.

of the table, drilling a slightly larger hole and inserting a new pin, corresponding to the size of the new hole. In the event of the surfaces of the joint itself becoming worn, the centre pin must be removed and the joint separated. The worn undersurfaces will need to be levelled with a sharp chisel, and pieces of veneer, preferably sawn cut or of similar thickness, glued on to build up a new surface. Leave overnight for the glue to set properly before trimming off the edges. The upper surfaces will now need to be levelled to allow the pieces to fit again. When this has been done, clamp the gate to the framework in the closed position and enlarge the pivot hole before inserting a new larger pin.

Surface damage usually requires the skill of the French Polisher and is dealt with in the chapters on repolishing (from page 53). However, the groundwork will need attention, and this must be done before any finishing can be attempted. Blistered or chipped veneers are typical examples.

When a **veneered surface** develops a blister it usually indicates that the glue under the surface has perished. In order to repair this, fresh glue must be applied. To do this, cut through the veneer with a thin sharp knife. An old hack-saw blade ground to a point and sharpened on both sides makes a very good veneer knife. When cutting through a veneer try to follow the grain so that the cut will not show when the repair is completed. When the cut has been made it will be possible to insert the blade of the knife under the surface of the veneer at either side of the cut. Bondfast glue can be used for this type of repair and it should be applied with the knife blade, getting in under the veneer surface wherever it is loose. A hammer can be used to put down the veneer, working from the outside edges of the blister towards the cut, where the excess glue will be pushed out. The surface should be wiped clean with a damp cloth. When the area has a firm surface the cut line must be taped to prevent the edges from curling as the glue hardens. Allow the work to stand overnight before starting to clean up. The tape will come off fairly easily if it is damped first. The surface should not need scraping, and this would be unwise if the veneer is thin. Fine sandpaper held firmly round a flat cork or block will clean up the surface, but be careful to restrict this to the area around the original blister so that you do not damage the surrounding surface.

Crossbanded veneers were often used as a decorative feature around the edges of tables, drawer fronts and doors of old furniture, and these are sometimes chipped or have pieces missing. A repair of this nature is comparatively easy, provided a suitable piece of veneer can be obtained. Cuts are made in the veneer just beyond the damaged area, cutting with the grain and using a thin sharp knife. The base area within the cuts must be cleaned of all old glue and veneer. A new piece of veneer should be cut to fit accurately into the space, and it should be cut about ¼″ longer than is required, thus allowing an overhang on the outside edge. The laying of the new piece can be done in either of two ways. (*a*) Using Bondfast glue and a hammer, the method for dealing with blisters, or (*b*) using Scotch or resin glue and a ‘G’ clamp. For this second method, glue is applied to the ground area, the veneer put into position and covered with a piece of paper, which in turn is covered by a flat piece of wood to act as a caul, and then a ‘G’ clamp is applied. The paper is used to prevent any glue which may penetrate the veneer from sticking to the wooden caul. When the glue has set the overhang on the edge must be trimmed with a sharp chisel, and the paper or tape cleaned from the top surface. If the veneer used for the repair was thicker than the original, then a cabinet scraper would be helpful in the cleaning up. If not, the sandpaper method suggested for the repair of a blister should be used.

Another type of damage to a veneered surface can easily occur when the veneer runs to the edge, and this will usually take the form of a piece being chipped out. In these circumstances a 'V' cut must be made to cover the area. The treatment is similar to that just described for a damaged crossband veneer, and the replacement piece may be glued in the same way. The cutting of a 'V' shape will usually mean that the cut will be at a diagonal to the grain instead of going across it and this will help to lose the line of the repair.

Chairs are probably the most ill-used pieces of furniture in any household. There are so many different kinds of chair, constructed in so many different ways, that any repair will naturally depend upon the individual circumstances. Often the trouble is simply joints which have worked loose, and if the repair is carried out as soon as possible it should not be a difficult task. An example of this is when the joints between the back legs and the seat rails have given way under the strain of someone continually leaning back in the chair and tilting it on the back legs (see Fig. 55). The same basic principles apply here as those mentioned for carcase repairs (page 31). Do not take apart more than is necessary. Corner blocks which are usually both glued and screwed, should be removed to enable the joints to be opened. These may be either mortice and tenon or dowels. If it is possible to open the joint completely without putting too much strain on other parts of the chair, all well and good. Any old glue must be cleaned out before attempting to re-glue. When it is not possible to take the joint apart, then it should be opened as much as possible, so that fresh glue can be worked into the opening. Whichever method is used, clamps will be needed to pull the joints up again. Clamping pieces will be required to protect the surfaces, and also to make sure that a square pull is obtained. It is generally necessary when repairing chairs to make specially shaped pieces to fit the legs or to cope with rounded corners or bends.

A more serious form of damage is a broken part such as a rail in an underframe. This can often happen when a chair has been used to stand on, or when children have been playing and climbing on these more flimsy sections. The rail should be removed, and a new one made using the original as a pattern. The main problem in a repair of this nature is to get the joints into place without straining other joints in the process. It is sometimes possible to spring the rail

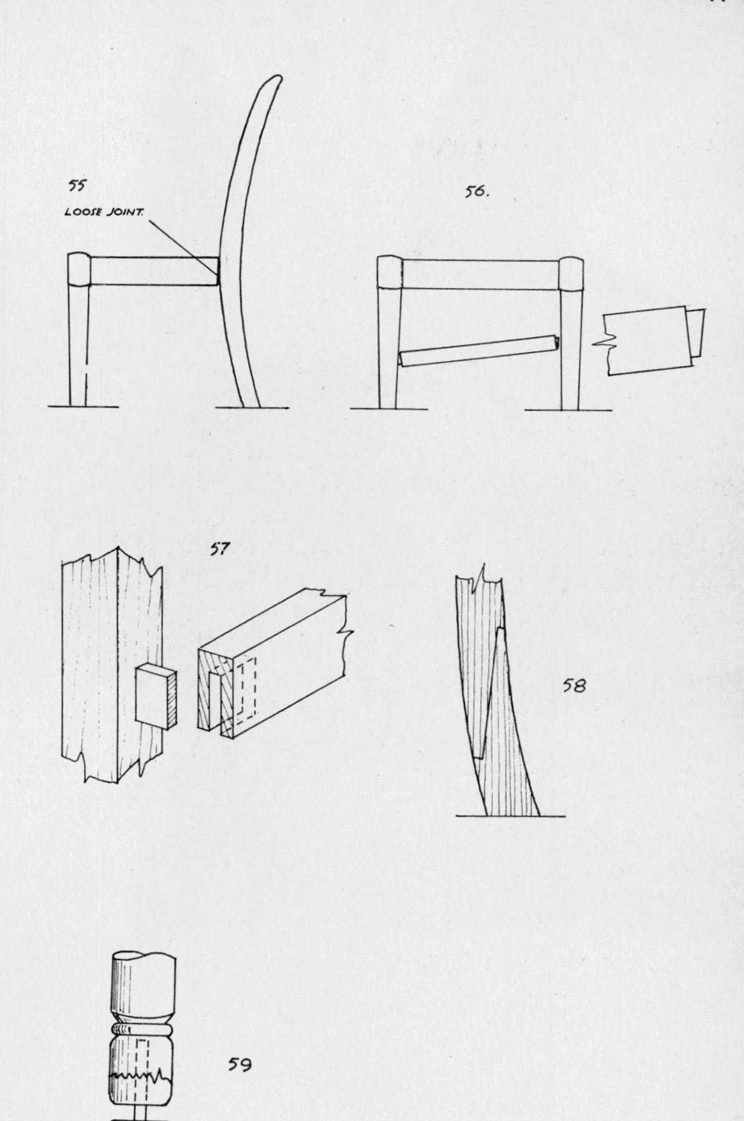

59

into place if the tenons are tapered (Fig. 56). If this cannot be done, then what is known as a loose tenon should be used. The loose tenon is made, fitted and glued into the leg. A mortice is cut into the rail and is open on the underside (Fig. 57). Glue is applied to the surfaces and the rail slid down onto the protruding tenon, where it should be clamped until the glue has set. In a very rigid framework it may be that this method will have to be used at both ends of the rail.

Chairs will often withstand very heavy knocks, but there are occasions when a leg may break. In the case of a square sectioned leg, it is generally preferable to splice on a new piece rather than attempt to glue the original piece back into place. Timber of the same kind or a very similar kind should be used. A diagonal or tapered splice is the most satisfactory method because this gives a greater glueing surface. If the ends are stopped (Fig. 58) there will be no tendency for the pieces to slip when clamps are applied. It is important when repairing a shaped back leg, that the splice should run with the grain. Extra strength can be given to this type of repair if the joint is screwed. This is done after the glue has set and the new piece has been trimmed to its finished shape and size. Holes large enough to take the screw heads are drilled into the new piece to a suitable depth, approximately 3/8″, and the screws inserted. Plugs are then cut from a piece of the same timber to fill the holes, care being taken that the grain runs in the same direction as that of the new part of the leg. The plugs are then glued, tapped into place, and the surface levelled off with a sharp chisel, and sandpapered after the glue has set.

A turned leg which has broken may at first appear more difficult to repair, but the following method should prove satisfactory. The broken ends are glued and put together, and then held until the glue has set. The leg is then cut off at a suitable place near the break (Fig. 59). A panel pin should now be knocked into the centre of one of the cut surfaces, and its head cut off with a pair of pliers or wire-cutters, leaving about 1/4″ sticking out. The two parts of the leg can now be brought accurately together and the end of the leg given a sharp tap with a hammer or mallet. The cut off end of the pin will mark the other cut surface, and with the pin removed both pieces have been marked for drilling. A 3/8″ hole should be drilled into each piece of the leg, at least 1″ beyond the break. A piece of 3/8″ dowel is cut to the required length, and a saw cut made along its length.

This cut should be widened to form a 'V' shape with the edge of a half-round file to allow excess glue and air to escape when the dowel is glued into the holes. Glue is applied to the dowel and the cut surfaces, and the parts brought together with the dowel forming a centre pin from the lower portion of the leg and up through the broken part into the upper sound section. The pieces should be held in place by a clamp and excess glue wiped off the surfaces. When the repair of a broken leg is being carried out, the leg will almost certainly have to be removed. Replacing the leg may require the tenons or dowels to be shortened a little so that it can be re-assembled more easily. Clamping in these circumstances can be awkward and a wire clamp or a clothes line used as a tourniquet will enable the joints to be pulled up. The surfaces and corners will need to be protected by the use of clamping pieces. If corner brackets had not been used in the original construction, additional strength can be given to the chair if they are made and fitted at this stage of the repair (Fig. 60).

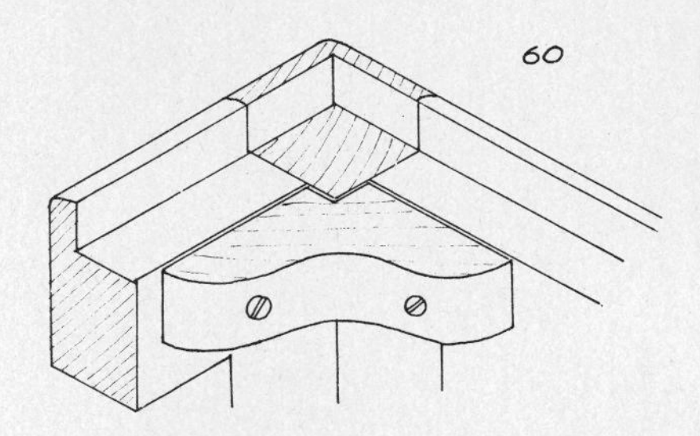

Broken **castors** can be an awkward problem. It may sometimes be possible to carry out a repair by soldering, if one has the facilities, or to have this done by someone else. If this is not possible, then a replacement will have to be found. It may well be that the only place to find an old-fashioned castor will be on a second-hand piece of furniture. This is one type of fitting which should always be salvaged whenever the opportunity arises. When dealing with this type of repair it is essential that the woodwork into which the castor or fitting is attached is sound. If not, this must be made good before any replacement is attempted.

The repair of the chair in photograph (Fig. 61) was a simple operation, yet the damage was unusual. The centre splat had been knocked out, damaging the bottom cross rail and breaking off a top corner and the tips of the bottom part of the splat itself. It was possible to re-glue the cross rail and rub-joint pieces of walnut onto the broken corners. When set the pieces were trimmed to the required shapes.

The top of the splat was located into the upper cross rail by means of a steel pin (a screw with the head cut off). The bottom had been held by a dowel which was broken. This was drilled out and a new piece of dowel was put through the rail and up into the splat. All old glue was carefully scraped off before the surfaces were re-glued, and the splat replaced, with the new dowel which was also glued prior to being tapped into place. The repaired back can be seen below (Fig. 61).

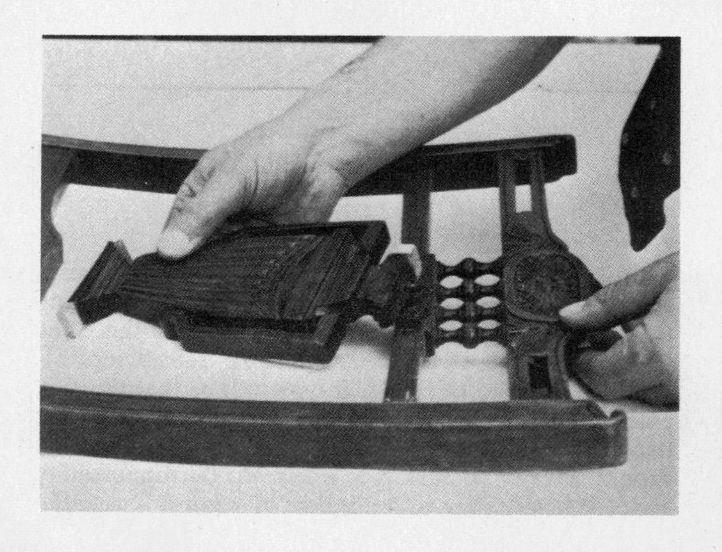

Fig. 61

PART TWO

REPOLISHING FURNITURE

CHAPTER SEVEN

TO DO OR NOT TO DO

How much repolishing one should undertake on an old piece of furniture will be determined largely by the type of piece in question. On a very old article it is desirable to retain the original finish as far as possible and simply clean and repolish to a minor degree. Even with a Victorian piece, where one might not expect to do much damage by stripping off all the old polish, one may very well find that unexpected problems have been created. For instance, Victorian and later furniture was often 'filled-in' with plaster-of-Paris which dried white in the grain but the whiteness was counteracted at an early stage by oiling with linseed oil. Subsequently the tint imparted by the applied polish, and perhaps by some additional colour, tended to mask the whiteness. If, however, the polish is stripped off after a number of years it will be found that the original oiling has ceased to be effective and the grain pores will show up white. This plaster-of-Paris will have been chemically cured by the water used in its application and it will now be quite impervious to stains or any other colouring matter. The only way of dealing with the situation is to brush out with a wire brush after wetting the wood, a laborious and not always one-hundred-per-cent effective process which may also tend to coarsen the surface and create other problems such as loss of detail, dubbed corners, etc.

This contingency will only apply, of course, when open-grain timbers are being treated. The commonest of these will be oak, ash, elm, mahogany and walnut. Where close grain timbers such as beech and birch are in question there will be no such problem.

The second reason for retaining as much as possible of the old finish is that colour matching is the most difficult of all the crafts associated with wood finishing. The colour of an old mahogany article, for instance, will be compounded of the original colour of the wood, stain, perhaps grain filler, the tint of the polish, subsequent fading —

not necessarily consistent throughout the article — and the penetration into the surface of the grime of years of wear, this grime often ‘fixed’ by the application of waxes, creams and other dressings.

There are good reasons therefore for retaining as much as possible of an old finish where the ‘patina’ of a well-worn article is to be preserved; this patina — a combination of colour and surface — to be simulated only where it is inescapable, i.e. where because of repairs the original wood has been disclosed.

With modern furniture the situation may not be as acute although many of the same factors are present. It is not always realised, for instance, that wood may darken or fade according to species and in some cases will fade after an initial darkening. But in the repolishing of modern furniture it is much more likely to be advisable to strip off the old finish after repairing than is the case with old pieces where the special character needs to be retained.

CHAPTER EIGHT

MATERIALS

The materials used in the polishing of furniture are many, varied, and to some people quite fascinating. Many of them can be a lifetime's study.

Where specialised materials are only obtainable from trade suppliers this has been indicated in the text. A number of materials, however, are now available from hardware and hobby stores and the home-improvement sections of large department stores.

Dyes. These are used as the colouring agent in most stains, in some cases to tint polishes, and to a certain extent paints. They produce transparent colours as opposed to pigments which are more or less opaque according to the amount used. Apart from their colour they are categorised for practical purposes by the solvent in which they most readily dissolve.

Water soluble, spirit soluble and oil soluble dyes are available *but it is frequently more convenient to purchase ready-made stains which may incorporate a number of solvents with the appropriate dyes.*

For tinting polishes and making up matching colours the most convenient dyes are the spirit soluble aniline dyes such as spirit blue, spirit green, spirit yellow, chrysoidine (orange), Bismarck brown (red) and spirit black.

Stains. Some spirit wood stains are straight dye solutions as already indicated. To prepare them it is wise to steep the crystals in methylated alcohol for 24 hours before use and then to decant into another container (glass or ceramic — not metal) through a filter paper or fine muslin. These solutions should be kept sealed and may be mixed to the desired colour as required. Usually not more than a quarter ounce of the crystals to a pint of methylated alcohol is required to produce the stock solution, though these proportions will not produce solutions of equal strength: very few grains of spirit green, for instance, will produce an appreciable colour in a pint of alcohol.

To these spirit dye solutions it is advisable to add a small proportion of a fixing or binding agent such as French polish in order to prevent the colour being easily disturbed by subsequent treatment. A dessertspoonful of polish to a pint of stain is adequate and should not be exceeded otherwise the stain will be difficult to apply evenly.

The most convenient way of purchasing water stains is by means of the textile dyes sold in capsules or small tubes. These, again, can be made up and stored in glass containers as stock solutions ready for mixing as appropriate. Most wood colours are variations on brown. Thus a medium brown dye solution to be used as a stain may be adjusted with very small proportions of red, yellow, blue, green or black to produce most of the shades likely to be required.

Another class of stain is loosely known as oil stain, the difficulty here being that, technically, the use of the word 'oil' has changed since the term was first used in wood finishing. For practical purposes any of the ready-made stains that can be thinned with Varsol may be deemed oil stains although other solvents may be present in addition.

In the same category are bituminous materials such as Brunswick black, Japan black and creosote which may be thinned with white spirit to make a cheap brown stain for some purposes. Only light browns should be attempted with these materials otherwise the residues may cause trouble with subsequent applications of polish and they may need 24-36 hours for drying.

The question of choice among the various categories of stains is not always straightforward. To assist the craftsman the following points are worth noting.

(*a*) Water stains are in general more light fast than other stains, are cheap and produce an even colour. The colours are usually dull and are therefore more appropriate for many repairs to old furniture. On the other hand their tendency to raise the fibres of the timber can cause complications though avoiding action may be taken (page 69).

(*b*) Spirit stains are convenient for colouring in small patches and may easily be added to polish for this purpose. They are, however, difficult to apply evenly over large areas and the colours are fleeting. They raise the fibres of the wood only to a limited extent.

(*c*) Oil stains are the easiest to apply but they are also the most penetrating. For this reason they should be applied sparingly and should never be used on soft woods such as pine and spruce, or hardwoods such as beech or birch where very patchy effects would result. It is essential that adequate drying time is allowed (24-36 hours according to conditions) before any coating is applied otherwise loss of adhesion may result.

One obvious, though very important, point should be made here: it is permissible to mix stains to achieve a specific colour but on no account should stains of different categories be mixed. The resultant mess would be quite useless!

In a special category is a group of staining agents which may be classified as chemical stains. These are bichromate of potash, lime, soda, caustic soda, ammonia, etc. In these cases the resultant colour depends on a reaction with the chemicals in the wood. Most of them will be considered when special finishes for oak are discussed (page 94).

Bichromate of potash is an exception because it is largely used on mahogany. It is, in fact, the traditional stain for this timber and produces a unique tone. The bichromate of potash is bought in crystal form and is dissolved in hot water at the rate of 2 ounces to 1 pint of water. This stock solution may be diluted as required. It should be borne in mind, however, that the final colour will not be apparent until the surface is quite dry and the reaction is finished.

Pigments. The most useful pigments for the polisher are the earth colours such as brown umber, venetian red, yellow ochre and burnt sienna, together with titanium white and gas black. These are used only in very small quantities, principally to modify colours based on transparent spirit stains, though some other uses will be indicated. If they are to be used to tint fillers it is convenient to buy them in tubes from an artist's supply store. They are also available in the form of 'tinters' currently used to tint the white-base of domestic paints. These are relatively expensive but are highly concentrated and only very small quantities will be required. Their special virtue is that they may be mixed with any medium.

Spirits. Care should be taken here to avoid confusion. Where used without qualification the term 'spirit' in the present context means methylated alcohol or methyl hydrate. 'White spirit', however, sometimes called turpentine substitute or 'turps. sub.', is a hydrocarbon and is quite different: it is, in fact, a light petroleum fraction or 'oil'. They are not interchangeable and confusion will cause wastage of materials and spoiled jobs.

French polish. This is a generic term covering a number of different varieties such as button polish (yellow), garnet (brown), pale (a light amber), transparent (not quite water-white) and white (a somewhat cloudy white). These may be modified by the addition of solutions of Bismarck brown to make a red polish or spirit black to make a black polish. Other spirit colours may be added for special purposes.

French polish is basically a solution of shellac in methylated alcohol and of the varieties mentioned transparent polish is the most generally useful and white polish should not be used except in special circumstances as will be indicated.

Oils. Linseed oil is the chief oil in this context but the two main varieties must be distinguished. *Boiled linseed oil* is used where an oiled treatment on the bare wood is required (see later instructions) and in the preparation of paste fillers. *Raw linseed oil* is used as a lubricant in the polishing process as will be shown. *White oil* is a mineral oil, a non-drying oil, often used as a basis for hair oil and is used as an alternative lubricant in the polishing process under some circumstances. *Teak oil* is a rather arbitrary commercial term covering what is really a thin, oleo-resinous varnish, the use of which is discussed later.

Waxes. Distinction has to be made between a wax used as a finish on wood and waxes used as dressings on an alternative finish. In the first case beeswax, one of the few animal waxes, is used. For light woods a bleached beeswax is available. Beeswax may be bought in flake form but if only block form is available it should first be grated.

The wax should then be covered with white spirit in a container and the whole heated in a water bath until the wax is dissolved. Waxes as dressings correspond to the wax polishes widely available commercially. The basis of these is often paraffin wax but with many additives, including silicone oils. In these circumstances it is not worth preparing one's own mixture.

Abrasives. There are a great number of abrasives in many forms that are useful in polishing processes. Steel wool may be obtained in grades ranging from No. 3 (coarse) to No. 000 (fine). The coarse may be used in the stripping process and the fine in dulling down a bright surface.

Flour pumice powder is used as an abrasive grit for dulling purposes, as will be shown. It is also sometimes used as an ingredient in fillers.

The most common abrasives are, of course, the abrasive papers. Normal cabinet glasspaper may already have been used in repairing. Garnet paper, nos. 180 and 220 are also useful where severe cutting down is required. Flour paper is a very fine grade of flint paper and is extremely useful, frequently with oil as a lubricant. The most generally useful abrasive paper, however, is wet-or-dry or waterproof paper. This is obtainable in a range of grades from 220 to 600. Usually the coarsest grade in normal usage is 320, with 400 or finer for the finishing touches. Either Varsol or soap and water may be used as a lubricant, the choice not being critical except in special cases.

Before attempting to fold or cut these papers, particularly the coarser grades, it is as well to wet them; otherwise they may fracture and cause scratching of the surface.

They should not be thrown away after only a little use but kept for later in a clean receptacle.

Strippers. Old polish may often be washed off with a hot, medium-strength solution of washing soda (1 lb. per gallon of water). In more difficult cases caustic soda may be used — but with very careful precautions. For small articles, however, or for small areas of a large article it is best to try first to soften and wash with methylated alcohol because soda tends to alter the colour of the wood once in contact with it.

Larger articles are best stripped by means of one of the patent strippers on the market. Some of the best of the modern finishes may prove to be impervious to these, and to most softening agents, in which case a methylene chloride stripper must be specified.

Metal fittings, after removal from the article, may be immersed in methylated alcohol.

Bleaches. The traditional bleach is oxalic acid which may be bought in crystal form and dissolved in hot water (2 ounces per 1 pint). It is a good cleaning agent and is useful for removing some ink stains, iron stains, etc. Oxalic acid may also be slowly dissolved in methylated alcohol and in this form has special uses. The acid is poisonous and the usual precautions in handling and storage should be taken.

Sodium hypochlorite is a useful bleach. This is the type used as a domestic bleach but is preferably obtained from a pharmacy in its concentrated form. It is especially suitable for taking out the red of some timbers such as mahoganies.

Where drastic bleaching of a timber is required the most satisfactory material is the patent two-component bleaching system now available. Component 1 or 'A' is an alkaline substance which tends to darken the timber. Subsequent application of component 2 or 'B', a peroxide, causes a severe bleaching reaction.

Fillers. Where a full finish is required on an open-grain timber it is an advantage first to fill in the pores with a paste wood filler. These may be purchased ready mixed at most hardware stores to various standard shades, light, medium and dark for oak, walnut, mahogany, etc. Fillers of the same brand will be intermixable for the achievement of specific shades and they may be thinned with Varsol. The resultant colour will depend partly on the filler but also on the initial colour of the wood and of any stain that has been applied. Except in one particular case, which will be noted, the woodfiller should always be just a shade darker than the timber. Transparent filler is useful stock since it can be modified to some degree by the addition of dry pigments.

Revivers and washes. A traditional type of wash for cleaning a polished surface comprises equal parts of water, paraffin, methylated alcohol, linseed oil and vinegar shaken together just prior to use to form a temporary emulsion. A little French chalk added to the mix converts it to a thin cream and assists the removal of all traces from the film. There are a number of commercial furniture creams available that clean and revive woods.

Where there is considerable dirt on an article it may be necessary to wash down with a weak soda solution followed by rinsing with clean water to remove residues.

For the care and maintenance of surfaces in the home a cream is better than a wax because of the cleaning action of the cream, whereas the wax leaves a deposit which, however slight, tends to hold dust. By far the worst practice is to use both indiscriminately according to the effectiveness of the advertisements. The result will be the accumulation of a sludge and a dull surface.

Acid catalysed lacquers. These are sometimes sold as 'plastic lacquers' (a singularly crude appellation). They vary in quality but the best may incorporate some melamine. They should be water-white and their hardening depends on the addition of an acid solution supplied with the lacquer. The recommended proportions of the mix should be adhered to. The resultant film should be heat, moisture and chemical resistant to a considerable degree. In some cases a one-component version of this type of material is available. This is known as a *pre-catalysed lacquer* and is convenient to use since no mixing is required but the quality of the film is not usually so high.

Polyurethanes. These are highly sophisticated materials with some special properties that may be usefully exploited. Both clear and pigmented versions are available and some of the most recent incorporate three classes of resins—alkyds, polyurethanes and silicones to achieve outstanding film qualities. They are available in gloss or matte finishes.

Nitrocellulose. A useful material primarily because of its fast drying properties. Better applied by spray than by brush, its film qualities are similar to those of French polish in that the film may be dissolved by strong solvents and may be softened by heat. Can be obtained in clear or pigmented form and most conveniently for small amounts in car touch-up packs.

Thinners. Any film-forming material may require thinning for one purpose or another. The important point to remember is that thinners are not often interchangeable. In some cases the thinner is a simple and readily available solvent, such as methylated alcohol for French polish or Varsol for household paints and varnishes. In most other cases the thinners consist of balanced solvent mixtures which should be obtained with each specific finishing material.

Brushes, small tools, equipment

Mops. The mop as illustrated (page 72) may be used for some coating operations and for colouring. It may be of bear's hair, squirrel or, the best, sable. Hog's hair mops are too coarse. A number 6 or 8 is useful for colouring purposes, while a number 14 is suitable for coating.

Pencil brushes. These are fine brushes suitable for touching-up and for picking out colour on small areas.

Paint brushes. 1″ and 2″ paint brushes are useful for a number of applications such as of stains and fillers. Used also for the application of catalysed lacquers. In these cases it is probably the best plan to buy the cheapest available and to regard them as expendable as it is very difficult to remove every trace of lacquer so that they remain soft.

Grass brushes. These are coarse, white, fibre brushes used especially for the application of bleaches and strippers which would destroy ordinary paint brushes.

Nail brush. Useful for brushing out residues from carvings, etc.

Dulling brush. A very soft brush employed for dulling on French polish and nitrocellulose surfaces. Obtainable from some hardware and artist supply stores.

Wire brush. Used especially for brushing out the grain of oak preparatory to liming treatment. A small, brass, wire brush as used for cleaning suede is also useful.

Quirk stick. This is a ⅜″ dowel stick about 6″ long, sharpened at one end like a pencil with the other end rather like a chisel edge as illustrated (page 70). It is useful for removing residue from corners and grooves after stripping or filling, and without risking too much damage to the surface.

Stripper knife. After the surface has been softened by the application of stripper it may be removed by the flat-bladed knife illustrated (page 65). It should be used in the direction of the grain and care should be taken not to dig into the surface.

Putty knife. For the spreading of stopper into holes etc. (page 97).

Miscellaneous items. Items such as a small penknife, a razor blade, a 1″ chisel, tins, jars and bottles will be required.

Some general points

All liquid materials should be retained in air-tight containers.

Containers should be clearly labelled.

Pouring should be away from the label.

All containers when not in use should be capped.

Nearly all the liquid materials referred to constitute a fire hazard and appropriate precautions should be taken.

The cleanliness of materials is important and contamination should be avoided.

Mops and pencil brushes, when first purchased, should be immersed in water or methylated alcohol for a few hours, taken out, shaken free of surplus moisture, the bristles pointed and left to dry.

Ideally, paint brushes should be regarded as expendable since it is very difficult to free them of every trace of lacquer after use.

CHAPTER NINE

GENERAL PROCEDURES

In this section the general procedures of wood finishing will be detailed. Subsequently their application to specific contingencies will be indicated.

Stripping. Where washing soda, or, particularly, caustic soda is used for stripping it should be applied by means of a grass brush. The utmost care must be taken in the handling of caustic soda. The flakes or pellets should be added to the water — *not* the other way round! Rubber gloves should be worn and any drops on persons or clothing avoided. The job is best done in the garage or in the yard. On no account should caustic soda be used on really old veneered work as it would soften the glue line and the veneer would come away.

Once the film is softened, whatever stripper is used, it is necessary to remove the residues. On flat surfaces this may be done by means of the stripper knife as illustrated in Fig. 62. Other surfaces may be cleared by the use of coarse steel wool.

The important point here is to let the stripper do the work as far as possible. If the stripper is left for a few minutes the surface should begin to blister. At this stage it is easily removed. If the blistering does not occur then the surface should be re-coated liberally and the same procedure adopted. The operator should not have to exert a great deal of force, incurring the risk of damage to the surface.

In the interests of cleanliness and the avoidance of damage to other surfaces it is good practice to have available some sheets of old newspaper when stripping. On these the residues can be wiped off the stripper knife, and the paper can then be folded up and disposed of — but bear in mind that the whole thing is now highly inflammable.

Finally it is essential to wash down in order to remove the last traces of finish and stripper, particularly where a wax is incorporated into the stripper. Commercial brands of stripper usually carry an instruction about this and the recommendations should be followed.

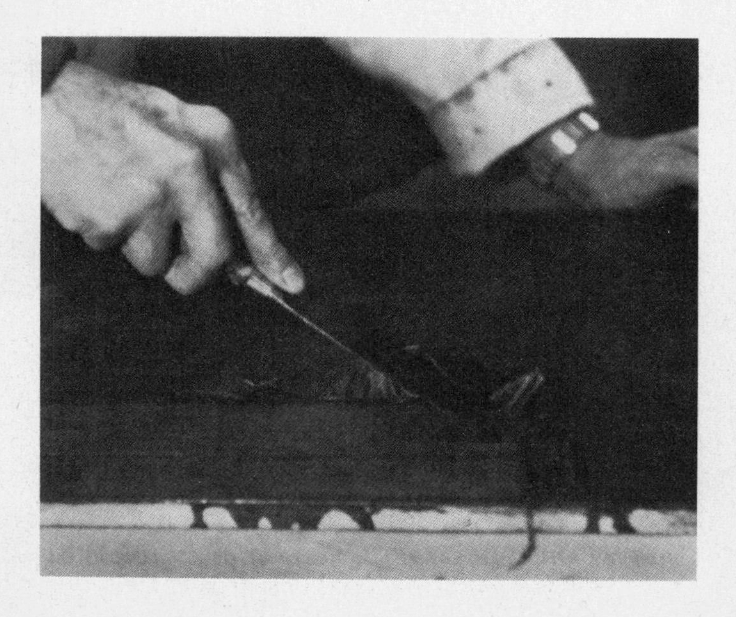

Fig. 62. Stripping off old polish. Note the angle of the stripper knife and the relatively clean ribbon of waste.

The general practice is to wash down with methylated alcohol and then to wipe dry.

Where caustic soda has been used the surface will have darkened considerably and it will be necessary, additionally, to bleach back to the original colour. A peroxide (No. 2 bleach) is the material to use and a fifty/fifty solution of water and peroxide is usually adequate.

Oiling. The oiling of timber may be undertaken simply in order to enhance the natural colour and figure of a choice piece of wood as in the case of burr walnut, Italian walnut, curl mahogany, etc. Sometimes this is undertaken after staining in order to enrich and darken the colour. End grain may sometimes be oiled in order to prevent the penetration of stain. Oiling is also a means of exposing the colour of the wood so that matching up may be undertaken. For instance, if oiling discloses a light streak not hitherto very evident, the oil should be allowed to dry and a thin film of polish applied. The light streak may then be coloured to match the remaining surface before any subsequent coating takes place.

The oil in question is boiled linseed oil and it should be applied sparingly, the residues being thoroughly wiped off with a clean, lint-free rag.

Where the oiling is undertaken in order to produce a finish and not simply for colour considerations the oil may be applied wetter. An old but clean flat brush is useful for the purpose, or a rag may be used. It is an advantage at this stage to paper in the oil. A 180 garnet paper is suitable and the oil should be papered in while wet, using the paper straight up and down the grain. This procedure will create something of a sludge which should then be lightly wiped off along the grain with a rag. After a drying period of at least 24 hours the surface may then be lightly papered with flour glasspaper along the grain and the residues removed. A further coat of oil should then be evenly applied and left to dry. An additional coat may be deemed to be necessary according to the porosity of the timber and the thoroughness of the cleaning-up. The most important factor is that each coat should be thoroughly dry before further applications.

The oil may be tinted if required by the addition of small quantities of tinters or oil soluble dyes or, with the loss of some clarity, a little dry pigment may be incorporated.

A variation may be introduced by the use of 'teak oil' instead of the linseed oil. In this case the build-up on the surface is likely to be quicker, say two coats instead of three, and the finish may be a little more resistant.

Finally, an oiled surface, when thoroughly dry, may be improved by a brisk rubbing or burnishing action using the back of a piece of glasspaper or even a screwed-up ball of brown paper (not newsprint). If a certain degree of roughness is apparent then this may be removed by rubbing with old flour paper prior to the burnishing.

Waxing. The beeswax paste referred to in the Materials section should be used for the waxing process. The method is substantially the same as for oiling except that papering-in is not normally required. Again the most important factor is the complete drying of one application before another is undertaken. Similarly the colouring agents employed with oil may be added to the wax, but in this case they should be added while the mixture is still fluid and should be well stirred in.

Where the necessity for matching up the colour is suspected it is a good plan to apply one rubber of French polish before waxing; match up with the appropriate spirit colours and proceed with the waxing operation when the colour is dry. A rubber of polish is also sometimes applied in order to hold up the wax, reduce the number of applications required and thus shorten the time required for the whole sequence.

Finally the surface may be burnished as for the oiled finish.

Staining. When applying stain to a large area it is extremely important to do it methodically by starting at one edge and proceeding to cover the surface so that there are no misses and only one edge to keep alive. (This provision applies, in fact, to all applications of liquid materials to surfaces and even to the simple act of dusting. Only by such methodical work can complete coverage be ensured.)

Applications of stain may be by means of a brush or by means of a swab of soft rag. For articles such as chairs or other items where there are quirks and corners to contend with a 1″ brush is convenient. In all cases, however, the most important point is to have available a separate piece of soft rag in order to wipe off surplus stain and even out the colour of the surface. It is also important that stain should not be slopped on too liberally or drying will be retarded and, in some cases, very ugly effects may result.

Where surfaces have been stripped it may be necessary in some areas to paper in the stain while it is wet in order to achieve penetration. Only fine paper should be used and the operation should be done with considerable care.

When the article has been stained it should be set aside in such a way that light and air can get to all surfaces. On no account should pieces be leaned one against the other or discoloration and patchy drying may result.

Normally the requirement in staining is that an even colour is to be achieved. In some cases, however, a quite different effect is required; the imitation of a worn and faded surface. One way of doing this is to apply the stain and immediately to wipe off in certain parts, say the middle of a panel, leaving the remainder longer to penetrate before lightly wiping off the whole. Another method is to stain uniformly and then to paper out the stain in certain areas. This has to be done carefully in order to avoid hard lines which would certainly not look authentic. A useful variation, having papered out the light areas, is to re-stain the whole with a diluted solution of the stain. This is particularly useful on carved work where the protuberances are 'highlighted' by papering of the stain back to the bare wood. A weak stain subsequently softens the contrasts and makes the effect acceptable.

Where modern pressed mouldings are encountered the shapes are so compacted by the process that the stain does not penetrate easily and it is a simple matter to wipe off the stain, while wet, from the high points. Even here, however, some judgment is required in determining precisely when to wipe off so as to avoid hard lines.

The most useful stain for these purposes is undoubtedly a water stain, and of these the Vandyke brown stain is most convenient. But there is much scope here for variation and experiment. For instance, a water stain, rubbed or highlighted, may be over-stained with a weak oil stain with good effect.

A widely used alternative method depends on the use of a pigment stain or 'sludge' to obtain the effect. Vandyke brown in powder form is first wetted and then by further additions of Varsol stirred into a paste of about the consistency of cream. To, say, a half-pint of this mixture a dessertspoonful of gold size should be added and well stirred in. This may be applied to the surface by means of a brush and then progressively spread and wiped off selectively according to the effect required.

The point about this method is that because we are here dealing with pigments rather than dyes there is not the same penetration. The effect is therefore easier to achieve. In addition, since the pigments tend to obscure slightly, the effect obtained is very similar to that resulting from the accumulation of dirt in corners and interstices over many years.

The colour of the sludge may be modified, for instance, by substituting brown umber, a lighter pigment, for the Vandyke brown or by the addition of a little gas black to produce a darker and colder mix.

Wiping off the sludge is the most critical part of this process and some delicacy is required. For the main removal an absorbent material is best, followed by a final light wiping with a soft cloth, taking care not to create hard lines. The timing of the operation is also important. The sludge should be at a crumbly stage for the best results.

Again there are possible variations. In some cases it is advantageous to apply a straight stain, fix it, when dry, by the application of a rubber of polish, then, after a reasonable interval, treat with the sludge as previously indicated. This has the effect of producing a cleaner colour where the sludge has been wiped. In this case it is most important not to apply too much polish, to allow it to harden thoroughly and to paper down lightly with flour paper before applying the sludge.

It is appropriate to establish here that water stains will swell the fibre of the wood. This will necessitate smoothing down with a fine garnet paper when the surface is dry and before proceeding with any other operation. This carries the risk of disturbing the colour too much and even taking it off altogether on corners and edges. A method of avoiding this is to wipe over the bare wood with water before staining, allow to dry then paper smooth. Subsequent application of water stain will then be found to raise the fibres very much less or in some cases not at all. This preliminary treatment is very desirable, especially on oak, where a water stain is proposed.

For the beginner it is a very good idea to try out some of these stains and procedures on odd pieces of wood before attempting to deal with a piece of furniture. It is important, however, that these sample pieces are properly cleaned up otherwise a false effect will be obtained.

Filling. One of the most important factors in filling-in the grain prior to polishing is that of colour (page 57). The filler will require thinning down with Varsol to the consistency of a porridge. It should then be applied methodically all over the surface with a rotary motion by means of a piece of hessian or coarse rag. This should be left for a few minutes until it is semi-dry and wiped off with a fresh piece of hessian, again with a rotary motion. Finally the surface should be lightly wiped up and down, with the grain, using a dry part of the hessian. The aim is to ensure that the grain pores of the wood are uniformly choked up and that the surface is free of all residues.

All corners and the quirks of mouldings should be cleaned of surplus filler by removing with a quirk stick as illustrated in Fig. 63.

The drying of the filler is quite critical in the wood finishing process. At least 12 hours should be allowed before proceeding to the next stage even though shorter times may be alleged to be safe.

Fig. 63. Using a quirk stick to remove residues of filler.

Failure to allow adequate drying time at this stage can result in serious defects such as white-in-the-grain, loss of adhesion, etc.

It is appropriate here, perhaps, to emphasise that it is not possible to be specific about drying times in relation to the volatile materials with which we are dealing throughout this section. Drying times are related to temperature and air circulation, factors which are rarely controllable.

Finally, having allowed the filler to dry, it is necessary to check that there are no residues. For this purpose the surface should be lightly papered with a piece of flour paper and the dust removed, taking care not to paper off edges and corners.

Bleaching. Care should be taken to ensure that bleaches are applied methodically over the whole area to be affected, using the grass brushes already mentioned. If a previously polished job is undertaken it may be necessary to paper in the bleach while wet in order to ensure penetration. In such cases it is necessary to protect the fingers with rubber gloves, except in the case of sodium hypochlorite.

By far the most important factor in bleaching, however, is the washing off afterwards. Some household brands of bleach carry an instruction to wash off with water or methylated alcohol and these instructions should be adhered to. An additional tip, however, is to anticipate the drying slightly (even though until the surface is quite dry it is impossible to be sure of the result) and wash off before the final drying. This is because if these chemicals crystallize in the grain they are not easily re-dissolved in the washing process but remain active in the wood fibres and can subsequently cause endless trouble, including violent changes of colour. Where oxalic acid is used it is customary to wash over with acetic acid or vinegar.

It must be emphasized that washing down should be effected with liberal quantities of water or methylated alcohol. Mere wiping over with a wet rag is not adequate. It will be apparent also that in these circumstances drying times are again important. Bearing in mind, in addition, that more than one bleaching operation may be necessary in some cases, it becomes clear that the procedure cannot be done in a hurry.

After the washing operation all surfaces must, of course, be wiped as dry as possible and must be left exposed to light and air.

On old veneered jobs it is not advisable to use the very powerful, two-component bleaches since the veneers are likely to have been put down with Scotch glue which is attacked by these chemicals.

Another contingency where bleaches are useful is where faded colours are to be simulated: first staining and then bleaching in order to kill some of the brighter tones.

French polishing. This is a skilled craft and cannot be learned from a book alone. Nevertheless, with practice and the guidance that can be given here it is possible for the novice to become sufficiently proficient for his purpose. In addition there are a number of variations of the polishing process and one or other of these may be found suitable both for the job in hand and for the degree of skill acquired by the operator.

Fig. 64. Brushing in a chair with tinted polish, using a mop.

Brushing. For many jobs having narrow members, for instance chairs, the initial application may best be by means of a brush (Fig. 64). Assuming the surface to be well-prepared and clean a coat of polish should be brushed on, using a soft mop. This should be done quickly but carefully and with not too full a brush. The polish should simply be laid on with no attempt to 'work' the brush, taking care not to allow the polish to overrun edges or to form pools in corners. One of the clues to successful brushing is the control of the pressure put on the brush throughout the stroke. However, if there are any excesses of polish or the polish froths up, this may usually be removed by going over the faulty part with the tip of the brush without further charging with polish.

If this is done cleanly the job may then be left for half an hour prior to re-coating in a similar manner. At the discretion of the operator, however, the surface may with advantage be lightly papered down between coats, using some old flour paper for the purpose. A little French chalk added to the polish in these initial stages will assist in subsequent papering-down or flatting.

The subsequent application of polish will be by means of the *polisher's rubber.* Larger surfaces such as flat panels are also best treated by rubber right from the beginning. It is therefore necessary at this stage to establish the nature of the rubber and the method of use, the use of the rubber being the special feature of French polishing.

The rubber is made of a pad of wadding or unmedicated cotton wool which acts as a reservoir for the polish, covered by a tautly wound piece of rag. The wadding, about 6″ square, is folded so as to assume a pear shape with a flat surface on top and a point at the front. When the wadding has been charged with polish the rag is placed over the flat of the rubber and folded over the front in such a way as to retain the point already made. The remainder of the rag is then given one or two more folds at the underside and finally twisted at the back to keep the whole in place (see Figs. 65-68).

The size of the rubber mentioned here is arbitrary but will be of average size. Two factors operate in this connection. To be comfortable the rubber must be convenient for the size of the craftsman's hand. Further it must relate to the size of the job being undertaken; it is not advisable to use a large rubber for a small job nor a small rubber for a large job. The skilled French polisher takes considerable care with his rubber and will not start a job until he is satisfied that it is in order.

He is also continuously checking this in use and having used it he conserves it in an airtight tin in order to retain its condition.

Charging the rubber is important. The polish is usually retained in a conveniently-sized bottle with a cork in which a slot has been

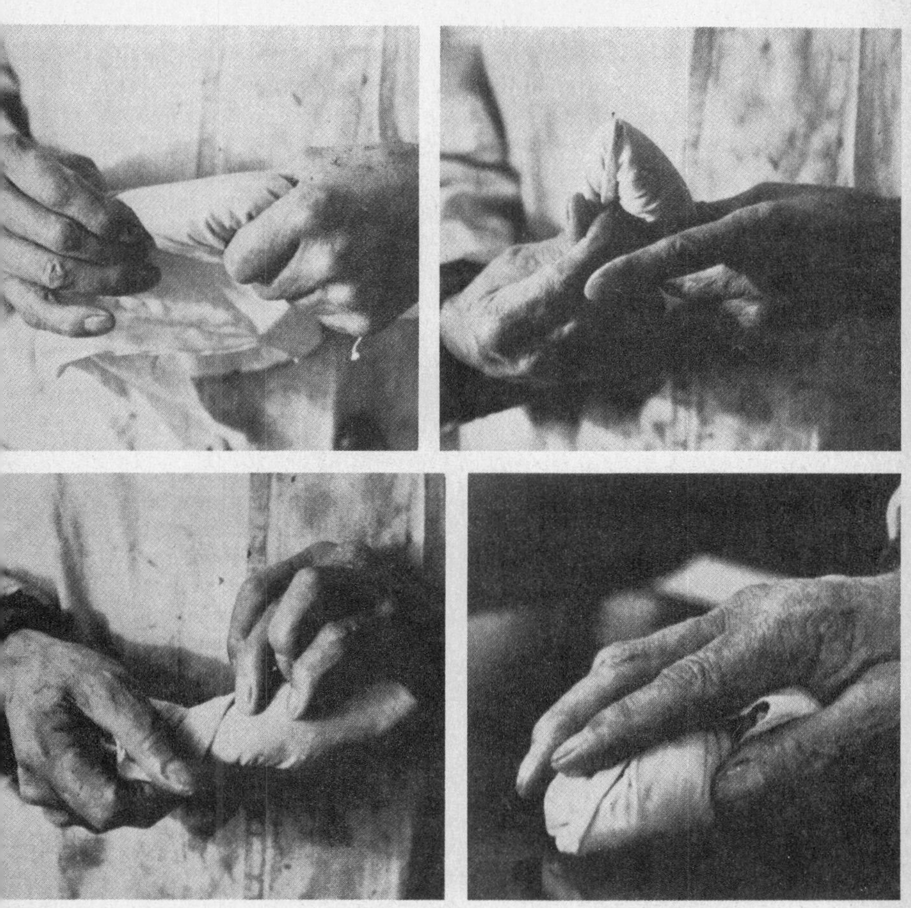

Fig. 65. The folded wadding is covered with the rag and shaped with the right hand to conform to the point.
Fig. 66. The rag is folded under, preserving the shape.
Fig. 67. The rag is finally wound up at the back and held in the palm of the hand.
Fig. 68. Applying the rubber to the workpiece. Note the fingers all the way round the rubber. Note also the dropped wrist. These two features make for even pressure over the whole face of the rubber.

cut. The polish is poured from this onto the rubber and it is essential to ensure that the polish is poured evenly over the face of the rubber. If this is not done then the polish will percolate through only one portion of the face of the rubber, the remainder will be relatively dry and will tend to pick up dirt and grease and will mar the surface.

The amount of polish to put into the rubber will vary according to its size, the size of the job and the stage that has been reached. In general the rubber must not be so wet that it becomes sloppy and that the polish oozes out of the sides. If the back of the rubber and the operator's hands are excessively sticky it is a sign that too much polish has been used. Too little polish is not such a bad fault but if insufficient polish is added to the rubber then, of course, the rubber becomes ineffective. Nevertheless, 'little and often' is a safe rule so long as sufficient polish is able to percolate through the rag onto the surface.

One general rule about the use of the rubber may be regarded as essential to success. It is that as the amount of polish in the rubber decreases the pressure must increase, thus ensuring that the rubber is dried out before re-charging. If this rule is not followed the likely result is that the rubber will become soggy and the surface sticky. If this happens the job should be left a while to harden.

It should be remembered that French polish dries solely by the evaporation of solvent and that therefore time has to be allowed for this to take place. For this reason French polishing is usually divided into three phrases: skinning-in, bodying and finishing.

Skinning-in is simply the application of a thin, preparatory skin of the French polish after the surface has been stained and filled or otherwise prepared and allowed to dry, any residues being smoothed with flour paper and dusted clean.

There are several variants of this first stage of polishing proper. The normal method is to charge a new rubber as already indicated and apply the polish straight up and down over the whole job several times with a light pressure, taking care to press evenly and not to force the polish into rivulets on the surface. Four or five passes over the whole of the surface will probably be sufficient for this stage of the process, the rubber being replenished with fresh polish as required. A thin film of polish will have been applied. It is now necessary to vary the path of the rubber in order to prevent the surface becoming excessively streaky and to pack the polish into the grain to the degree required. In order to do this without churning up the soft polish it is necessary to lubricate the surface by dipping a finger into an oil pot and applying a little oil from the finger to the surface being treated. It must be remembered that oil in this French polishing process is a necessary evil and only just so much oil should be used as is essential for the purpose.

Either of the two types of oil may be used: raw linseed oil or white mineral oil (page 58). The choice is really one of personal preference and of availability although there are other factors that need not be investigated here. The principal consideration is that neither oil should be used to excess or faults will develop: 'sweating with the white oil and 'cracking' with the linseed oil.

Using the oil as a lubricant in the manner indicated it is now possible to proceed with the rubber, using a circular motion as indicated (Fig. 69). Starting at the top right-hand corner proceed methodically to the extreme left, keeping the rubber in contact with the surface. Do not lift the rubber but return with the same motion to the extreme right at a slightly lower level and so on until the whole of the surface has been covered. At this point the rubber should be lifted, returned to the original starting point and the whole routine repeated until a satisfactory film has been achieved. At some stage it will be found necessary to add a little more oil but this will be determined by the size of the surface and the amount of polish with which the rubber has been charged. It is not good practice to use a wet rubber and the consequent use of a great deal of oil to prevent sticking. At this stage, too, the previous recommendation to increase the pressure as the rubber becomes drier should be brought into effect.

Occasionally it is wise to change the routine by using the rubber straight up and down the surface in order to eliminate the rubber marks. After this the routine may be continued as before.

When it is assessed that an adequate, initial film has been applied the work should be laid aside. There are no measurable standards by

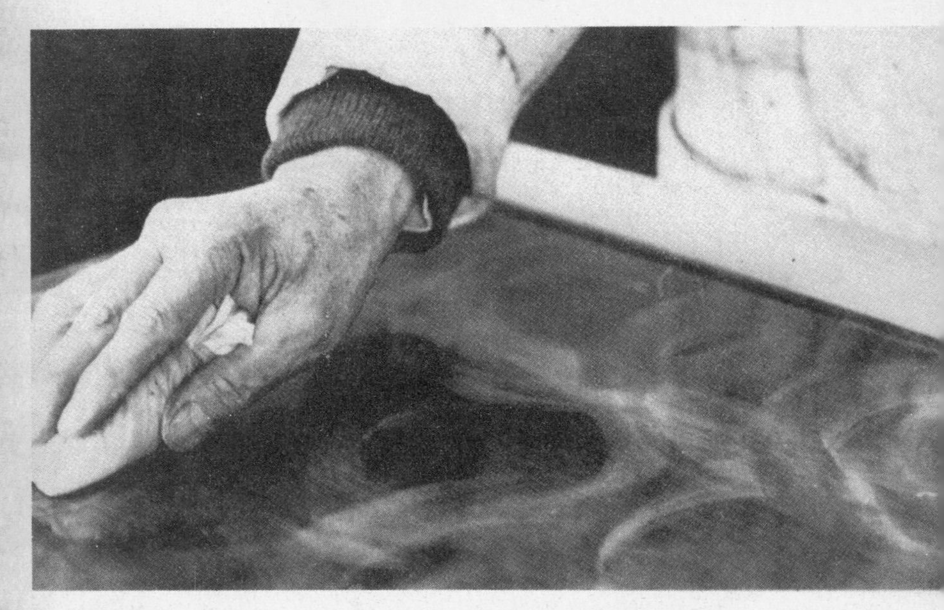

Fig. 69. The circles simulate the path of the rubber in action and the flash of the oil smear.

which the polisher may judge when to stop. The aim, however, is to apply a film which is flat and which will be a sufficient basis for the sort of finish required.

Fadding. A variation of this 'skinning-in' process is known as "fadding-in'. For this purpose an old rubber is taken and the rag removed. The wadding thus exposed is charged with polish in the normal way and the 'fad' is applied straight up and down as, previously, with the rubber. In this case there is no question of employing the rotary motion or of applying pressure. The polish is simply laid on in a straightforward manner. The special usefulness of this method of application arises where small members, quirks and corners have to be treated, the fad making contact with such surfaces much more readily than would a rubber.

Grinding-in. Still another alternative to skinning-in is 'grinding-in'. This is especially appropriate where a thin but hard and full finish is required, which is often the case with repaired portions of good quality cabinet articles. The technique here is first to dilute the polish considerably: ten parts of spirits to one of polish. This is used to charge as old and compact a rubber as can be found. A coarse rag is used to cover the wadding: a piece of twill or sailcloth is suitable. After a few initial passes along the grain the rubber is used in close circles in the manner previously indicated. Little if any effect will be noticed immediately but gradually a sheen will develop. Preferably no oil at all should be used and the rubber should be charged very sparingly. If this is done without making the surface sticky then it is safe to proceed to the next stage which is to dust some flour pumice powder onto the surface of the wadding before again covering with the rag. This combination of thin polish and pumice powder applied as indicated will produce a rock-hard, preliminary surface that is a first-class basis for any finish.

If in the course of any of these methods of application it is found that a portion of the surface has gone duller than the rest, it is important not to seek to remedy the fault by paying extra attention to that area. On the contrary that area should be neglected for a while. When it has hardened off it will respond to the normal application.

The first stages of polishing, then, may be by means of brushing, skinning-in, fadding-in or grinding-in. To obtain the best value from these processes there should now follow a drying period which may be as short as an hour but preferably longer. The surfaces may then be lightly papered down with flour paper, using a little oil as a lubricant.

At this stage it is sound practice to deal with any surface defects and any rectification of colour that is necessary. These procedures will be discussed later (page 82). (It is convenient here to continue with the actual polishing process.)

Bodying. After the initial coating the next stage is that of 'bodying'. This is, in effect, simply a continuation of the technique described for skinning-in. The aim is to build up a sufficient body of polish on the surface, the requisite film thickness. Each rubber should be worked out quite dry with increasing pressure so that a hard, relatively dry flat surface results. The size of the rings made by the rotary motion should be increased and the periodic straightening-off should completely eliminate the previous rubber marks.

It is possible to proceed directly from bodying to finishing in some cases but it is usually an advantage to allow the surface to dry out and settle down. In this case the surface must be wiped clean and any surface defects finally eliminated. This may necessitate papering down but only the oldest paper with little cut in it and well lubricated should be used. It is essential to avoid coarse scratches at this stage. An alternative method is to use a piece of felt which is fed with oil and flour pumice powder for this final flatting. The sludge must then, of course, be wiped off, leaving a clean surface.

Stiffing-up. Two methods of finishing are available. The most generally useful is the "stiffing-up' process. The procedure is to charge a rubber which is not too hard or compacted and to continue working up the surface as in bodying but with rather larger sweeps and more delicate pressure. The aim should be to eliminate the tracks of the rubber with each succeeding pass. The rubber should be frequently re-charged but the utmost control over the wetness of the rubber and the degree of pressure should be maintained. It should be remembered that the surface is by now extremely sensitive and that the end of the process is in sight.

The rubber should now be directed straight up and down the surface, still with a light pressure, with the strokes overlapping so as to cover the whole surface. At the end of each stroke the rubber should be allowed, where possible, to go half over the end of the piece before reversing the direction. The rubber should not be lifted nor should the turn be made within the edge of the piece. This is the most critical part of the process. If it is done correctly the result is a clean, flat, bright finish, free from oil.

The rag used to cover the rubber should be of well-washed, soft linen such as old sheeting. Some polishers modify the process by introducing a little methylated alcohol and thinning down the polish. This tends to reduce the harshness of the finish but requires more skill because of the more powerful solvent action.

Spiriting-out. Spiriting-out involves a different approach and produces a refined, hard, more closely-knit surface which at its best is like glass.

After the bodying stage the rubber is charged with a fifty/fifty mixture of polish and methylated alcohol. The rubber should be an old, compacted one and should be covered with a fairly coarse, tough linen. Some flour pumice is frequently added to the inner surface of the rubber which should then be fairly liberally charged with the half-and-half mixture.

Frequently this one charge will be sufficient if the surface is already well bodied and no scratches are apparent. Only a light pressure should at first be applied so that the transfer of polish from the rubber to the surface is almost imperceptible. Gradually the pressure should be increased until the rubber is quite dry. A little oil will be necessary in the early stages but as the rubber becomes drier and the surface harder no more oil need be added.

The application of well-regulated pressure is crucial to the success of this procedure. Too often it is assumed that because a fine surface is to be achieved it is necessary to treat it delicately at this stage. The reverse is true and a skilled polisher will often resort to two-handed pressure at this critical stage rather than risk a reduction of pressure.

When the rubber is fully dried out the surface should be hard, bright and without blemish. There will, however, be a slight smear from the oil. This smear may be removed by leaving the surface to become hard overnight and then lightly polishing with a household furniture cream.

Alternatively the spiriting-out process may be carried a stage further. For this purpose an old rubber from which all polish has been washed with methyl alcohol and which has been allowed to dry is covered with a piece of soft linen or damask. A few drops of methyl alcohol are added to the face of the rubber which is then rubbed on the back of the hand or forearm until most of the 'wetness' has been dissipated. The rubber is then applied to the surface with a light brisk motion until the smear of oil disappears. It may be necessary to repeat this process if the smear is not completely removed in this one operation but great care must be exercised to ensure that the surface is not wetted too much or the surface will be burned. Following an interval of time for drying, a light rub with a cream may prove desirable to obtain the maximum, permanent gloss.

Dulling down. The gloss finishes produced by French polishing are frequently unacceptable unless the gloss is modified to some degree. The first requisite is that the surfaces should be allowed to harden thoroughly. The usual method, then, is to take a dulling brush (Fig. 70) comprising very fine, soft hair, dust on to it a little flour pumice powder and brush this carefully backwards and forwards the length of the surface. In this way a very fine abraded matte finish is obtained if the scratches are kept perfectly straight with no criss-crossing at any point. Where dark woods are being treated it is sometimes advisable to mix a little gas black or charcoal dust with the pumice in order to prevent any residues lodged in crevices from showing up.

A duller effect may be obtained by abrading the surface with a piece of felt soaked in a mixture of half Varsol and half oil and on which some pumice powder has been sprinkled. For treating mouldings and other small members wadding may be substituted for the felt. The Varsol/oil mix may also be used with the brush.

An alternative method is to use the finest grade steel wool (000

Fig. 70. Dulling down with brush and pumice powder.

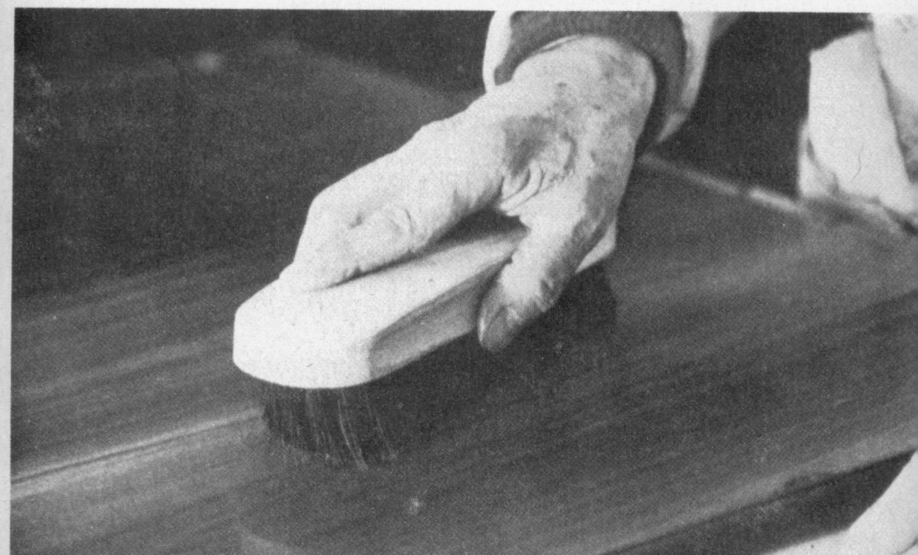

or 0000) with soap and water as a lubricant. On the hard finishes that will be dealt with later the steel wool may be used dry, i.e. with no lubricant, or a mixture of wax and Varsol may be used as a lubricant. When the resultant sludge is wiped off, the surface should have a very choice visual and tactile effect.

Surface defects. Veneer faults and repairs have been dealt with on page 44. Solid areas that are bruised can be dealt with before polishing. The bruise should be covered with a small piece of wet rag and a hot iron applied. This will swell the fibres of the wood and may raise the indentation to the general level. In some cases it will be necessary to repeat the procedure. When the surface has been allowed to dry it should be papered flat, using, say, 180 garnet paper.

The end of an old file placed in a gas flame may be used for this sweating-up procedure. Alternatively an electric soldering iron may be used.

Indentations that are too deep for this treatment will need filling. The traditional method of effecting this is to melt some solid shellac

Fig. 71. Running in a piece of shellac with a hot iron.

into the hole by means of a hot iron, the molten shellac being lightly pressed in by a wetted finger (see Fig. 71). The result should be slightly protuberant and the excess should be trimmed off with a sharp chisel, finally being lightly papered. A piece of button shellac is required for this purpose.

Where the bottom of an indentation is smooth it is a good plan to prick this a number of times with the point of a penknife before filling. This helps to provide a 'key' and minimize the chances of the filling falling out at a later stage if shrinkage should occur.

Other methods of filling holes and bruises are best left until the skinning-in stage has been completed and the surface has hardened.

Of the materials available for the filling of small holes at this stage perhaps the most satisfactory is cellulose 'jam'. To prepare this take a shallow tin lid and cover the bottom with cellulose lacquer. This should be left overnight and a further small quantity added,

Fig. 72. Cleaning off the residues of cellulose 'jam' with a razor blade. Note the firm grip at the bottom of the blade.

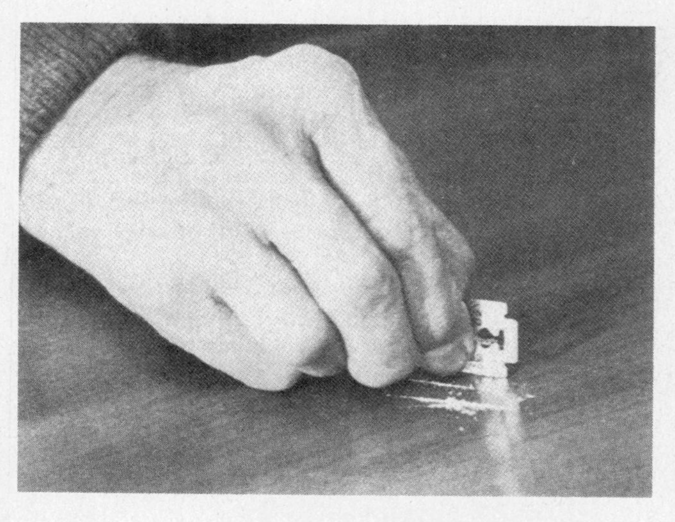

covering the surface. The same procedure should be repeated daily until the lid is full. The material will gradually dry out, with the middle likely to remain slightly softer than the outside edges. It is at its best for the present purpose when it is at the consistency of Cheddar cheese.

To fill the hole a little of the jam should be taken up on the point of a penknife and spread into the cavity, open joint or bruise. Some pressure will be required and very little residue should be left on the surface. The residue is removed immediately by taking a razor blade at right angles to the surface and scraping backwards and forwards with a firm pressure. It is essential that the razor blade is held firmly at the bottom and that it is not allowed to flop about out of the vertical (see Fig. 72). It is important, too, that the scraping off should begin immediately after the application of the jam and before it has had time to harden further.

The advantage of this method of filling holes is that the material is transparent and therefore does not create a problem of matching up for colour.

Beeswax or Japan wax may also be used to fill up the smaller holes. The wax is simply rubbed in and the residues scraped and papered off. If colour is required a little dry pigment, such as brown umber, is picked up on the wax and rubbed in.

There are a number of 'plastic woods' available on the commercial market. These come in cans or tubes and dry quite rapidly to the consistency of wood. They can be filed, sanded, nailed, etc. The only problem is the colour. If a test reveals the colour suited to the job at hand then it can be used with confidence.

It is useful to remember for some contingencies that any filling material such as china clay, barytes, silex or wood flour can be bound with French polish, cellulose lacquer or even epoxy resin glue plus a little pigment to make a useful filling or stopping material Fillers such as 'Polyfilla' and asbestine are too course for the purpose.

One warning is perhaps worth noting. It is possible to start with a hole to be filled and to finish up with a bump where residues have not properly been cleaned off, the cure being worse than the disease.

Finally in this context, where it is required that the authenticity of a really old and valuable article should be preserved it is not desirable to eradicate all surface blemishes. Only the most offensive faults or those which detract from satisfactory usage should be attempted.

At the other extreme the faker who imitates old furniture, not simply for aesthetic effect but in an attempt to deceive, actually bruises and mars the new wood deliberately with chains and a variety of gadgets.

One surface blemish that is frequently encountered is the ring mark made by a wet and/or hot receptacle. Where the job is not to be stripped and the marks are mild they may sometimes be removed by friction. This will be assisted if the surface is first treated with camphorated oil (available at most pharmacies). There is also a patent mixture on the market in paste form. In severe cases the treatment is more drastic. First wipe over the affected part with white oil. Then lightly wipe over with methylated alcohol and set fire to it. The surface will be re-fused and the mark removed. It need scarcely be said that this is a tricky operation to be performed with great care, particularly in seeing that the rag used for applying the alcohol is removed before setting fire to the surface. Similarly the bottles containing the oil and the alcohol should be well out of the way and it is best to do the operation away from carpets and other inflammables. The function of the oil is to protect the surface from the naked flame and it is possible to do the job so that all that is further required is to clean up with a reviver.

Additional points to note are that the surface should be clean before attempting this procedure otherwise contaminants may be burned into it: speed is required in applying and lighting the spirit since it is very volatile and will evaporate in a few seconds: and it is a safeguard against too drastic action for the flame to be blown out just before it peters out at the edges.

Colouring. As has already been established the colouring process may start with the application of a stain with cumulative modifications through the use of fillers and tinted polishes. The end result of these procedures and applications should be the desired colour. But discounting accident and human failure there are two causes for discrepancies in colour: the first is variation of colour in the original piece of wood from which the article is made and the second is some interference with the surface due to the carrying out of repairs.

The colour to be used will be of the type described on page 55, matched to the required tone but slightly lighter than the end colour required. The brush to be used may be a pencil brush, a No. 6 or a No. 8 mop, according to the size of the area to be treated. Having dipped the brush into the colour, most of it should be eliminated by drawing the brush between the forefinger and the side of the colour pot, thus ensuring that it is not too wet. The brush should then be applied to the area, taking care not to overlap the part which does not need treatment. Even, steady strokes of the colour brush should now cover the whole area, again with no overlapping. It is important not to go over the same area more than once while the colour from the first stroke is still wet. When this is dry, however, the procedure can be repeated until the required colour is obtained, using the brush delicately. Part of the necessary control of the brush in this operation

Fig. 73. Using a mop for coating with colour.

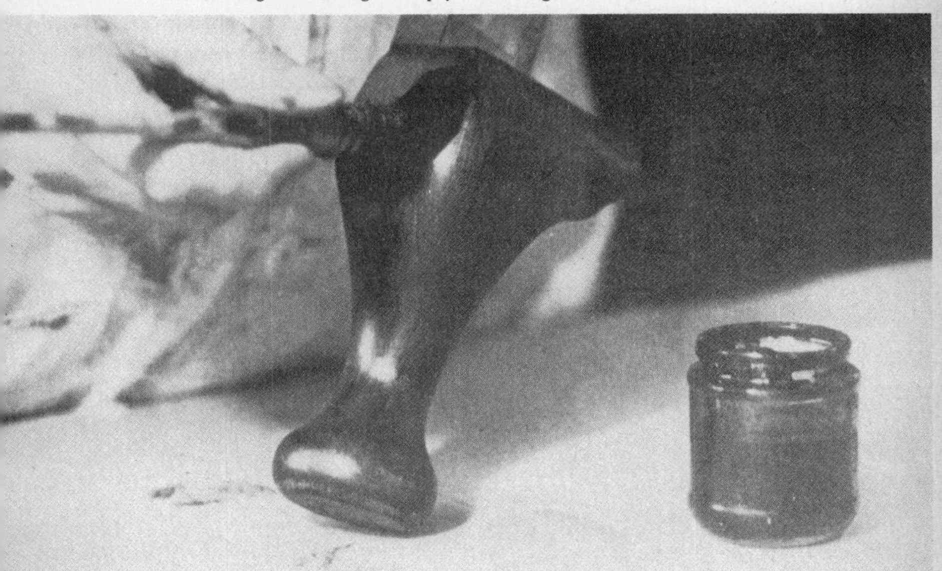

is the angle of the brush and the pressure applied. In general only the tip of the brush is used and with only a light pressure (see Fig. 73).

Sometimes when dealing with such repair work it is found that although the colour made up is correct in terms of tone and density it is too bright (in the colour sense, not in the sense of surface brightness). In this case it may be desirable to add just a trace of pigment. Brown umber or yellow ochre or a mixture of these may be suitable in some circumstances. In other cases a trace of grey (gas black and titanium white) may be more suitable. A little pigment in the colour will also help to obtain an even effect. The quantity of pigment used, however, must be minimal because the more pigment used the more opaque the colour will become.

Where complete but relatively narrow parts of an article are to be coloured it is possible to adopt a different technique. A piece of new wadding should be soaked with the colour and drawn once firmly over the area. In this case the colour has to be just right because there is no possibility of repeating the operation. It is also advantageous for this purpose to add just a little more polish to the colour as a binding agent.

Another method of applying colour is to use a small but old rubber with a soft, linen cover and charge it with a rather dark colour of the appropriate tone. Most of the colour should be squeezed out of the rubber and a spot of oil put on the face of it. This should be worked straight up and down the surface, gradually and evenly changing the colour. The essential factor here is even distribution so as to avoid the creation of patches.

A special aspect of colouring is where a pronounced figure has to be imitated, say on a piece of sap walnut. In such a case it is first of all necessary to match the background colour. Then a different and darker colour will be required for the distinctive markings usually denoted as the figure. For this operation a pencil brush or small mop is required and only the tip should be used in applying the colour (see Fig. 74).

It is not usually possible to match up a colour satisfactorily if the surface is dull. If prior to colouring a surface has been papered

Fig. 74. Touching up with a pencil brush.

down or otherwise dulled, therefore, it is usual to wipe over the surface with a polish rubber (free of oil) so that the colour of the surrounding area can clearly be seen.

Once the colouring has been achieved it is necessary to fix it. This is done by one or two passes of the polish rubber, not too liberally charged and with a touch of oil on it. Only when this is dry and the surface lightly papered with old, oily flour paper should one proceed with the bodying. The essential point is to avoid disturbing or washing off the colour that has been so carefully applied.

The general rule as to when the colouring operation should be undertaken is that it should be done in the early stages so that there is a maximum protection by means of the subsequent body of polish. It is also a rule not to colour until a surface of the requisite quality has been achieved. Both these requirements are met if the colouring is done after skinning-in and after the rectification of surface faults such as bruises etc.

Colouring, as with all polishing processes, is usually most conveniently done where the article can be to some extent dismantled and processed on a bench. But with colouring the final check must be with the part in place. A colour that is correct seen on a horizontal plane may appear wrong in the vertical position.

One special warning is relevant here. An increasing proportion of cheap and medium priced modern furniture is 'grain-printed', i.e. an exotic grain pattern is printed on a plain timber or on a pigmented undercoat. Thus any repair which disturbs the surface is likely to disclose a background quite different from the rest of the surface. To restore this may require considerable skill but the methods proposed here will be adequate. The main points are, first, to make sure the surface is without blemish, second, to obtain a matching background and third, to imitate the special features of the print.

CHAPTER TEN

WORKING WITH MODERN MATERIALS

Modern materials such as **acid catalysed lacquers** and **polyurethanes** may be used to advantage in certain circumstances. Their predominant virtue is that they provide a surface that is much more resistant to the everyday hazards of wear, heat and spillage than is French polish.

Acid catalysed lacquers and **polyurethanes.** It is not good practice normally to apply these materials to older finishes. They are therefore most useful for new work or where the previous finish has been wholly removed.

Procedures for staining and filling are the same as under French polish, with the proviso that it is wise to ascertain from the supplier that all the materials are compatible.

Both of these materials can be expected to have excellent film properties but while the acid catalysed lacquer (A.C. for short) is water-white the polyurethane will have a yellowish cast. For some purposes this will not be disadvantageous: it may even be an advantage. On the other hand, with light timbers, say, natural oak, the A.C. lacquer is better in terms of colour.

Both A.C. and polyurethane will give a high gloss finish from the brush, the polyurethane particularly so, but a brush finish is not good enough for furniture. For this reason these materials are usually finished by first flattening with 180 garnet paper and then with 000 steel wool with a little wax dressing, both the abrasive paper and the steel wool being used up and down in the direction of the grain.

Experience shows that the best way of applying these materials is to thin them down with, say, 10-15% of the appropriate thinners. When the first coat is dry and lightly papered, any colouring or making good should be done. Further coats of the thinned material may then be applied according to the thickness of the film required.

It will be seen that with these materials there is much less of a requirement for skilled manipulation since no rubber is used. On the other hand they are not universally appropriate for all types of repair and surface treatment.

CHAPTER ELEVEN

SPECIAL JOBS AND FINISHES

Gilding. The best 'gold' finishes are, of course, achieved by the application of gold leaf, a craft not dealt with here. For the rest, they are done by means of metallic powders, usually called bronze powders. Many shades of gold are available but it is likely that even the nearest that can be found in matching an old gilded article will require adjustment.

This can be done by adding the appropriate colour to the mix of bronze powder and binding agent or by applying the new bronze and subsequently treating with a sludge in the manner already described (page 68).

A simple gilded article with no repaired surface should be washed down with detergent and allowed to dry prior to coating. Ready-mixed bronze paints are available but there is little choice of shade and they are all oil based, which limits subsequent treatments. Similar limitations apply to aerosol sprays.

An alternative plan is to take some bronze powder, wet it with the appropriate thinner and then add the binding agent. At this stage any additional colouring agent may be introduced so long as it is compatible. If any doubts exist about this then dry pigments will be perfectly safe.

If a quick-drying finish is required it is best to use a clear nitrocellulose lacquer as the binding agent although this will necessitate slick application. For a slower-drying finish the binding agent should be a gold size or a pale oil varnish. In such cases the initial wetting and mixing of the powder will involve the use of Varsol.

Application by brush should be done carefully, avoiding pools and overbrushing otherwise a shadowy effect will result. It is always worth while to apply a clear coating over a bronze finish in order to prevent or at least delay tarnishing.

If, after the bronzing, any antiquing is undertaken, then a finishing coat is of course essential. In this case an oil-based material is not suitable for either coating since this would pick up the sludge.

One material to be avoided here is an A.C. lacquer which is liable to cause tarnishing.

'Silver' or 'aluminium' finishes are treated similarly and in spite of previous warnings it can be said that the ready-mixed metallic paints now available in the shops are very much improved and useful for straightforward jobs.

As with any sort of colouring, care should be taken to ensure a basis of a fine, smooth texture before coating, otherwise the finish will appear coarse. A damaged gilt frame, for instance, may require building up with plaster at some points. This should be smoothed down with fine paper and coated with shellac. More than one coat may be necessary in order to build up a smooth, non-porous surface suitable for gilding.

In addition it will probably appear that the original background was yellow in order to enrich the final colour of the gilt. It will make the possibility of a close simulation of the colour more likely if the colour of the background is first reproduced.

Limed oak. A paste made of garden lime (slaked lime) and water may be brushed on to oak and allowed to dry. The residues are then papered off with fine glasspaper and the surface cleared. It will be found that the wood has been stained a distinctive greyish brown and that the lime remains white in the grain pores. This is the limed oak effect. It is good practice, however, prior to applying the lime, to brush out the grain with a wire brush in order to enlarge and equalize the cavities.

The traditional practice is to try to fix the lime in the grain by the application of white polish but it is extremely difficult to obtain consistent results. A simpler method is to take a modern transparent filler and work in some titanium white: fill the grain with this, wipe off and leave to dry in the normal manner.

When the residues from this operation are cleared by papering the surface may then be protected by a coat of white polish or acid catalysed lacquer. Finally it is customary to dull down the surface to produce the most acceptable result.

Surfaces of this type that need repairing are usually sad-looking affairs where the white in the grain is sullied in patches. The surface should be wiped over with detergent solution and, when quite dry, the grain should be brushed out with the wire brush. Any necessary colour adjustments to the surface may then be made and the grain filled in as previously indicated.

Weathered oak. The treatment here, which aims to imitate the silver-grey effect on exposed oak and ash palings, is similar to that for limed oak except that in this case the lime is mixed into a solution and allowed to settle. The liquor is then decanted and used to treat the timber. When this is dry the colour needs to be protected but there is no attempt to fill in the grain.

The colour obtained by this process is very delicate and easily spoiled by the coating.

Pickled pine. Pine has often been used as a substrate for painting and gilding but is also attractive in itself. It tends to yellow on exposure and any clear finishes applied should, preferably, themselves be water-white and non-yellowing.

Pickled pine is the result of a chemical treatment producing beautiful contrasts between the spring and summer wood. First add one part of nitric acid to eight parts of water (do *not* add water to the acid). With the usual precautions for both operator and surroundings, coat the pine surface evenly and leave to dry. A light papering with flour paper is followed by a further staining with a weak solution of bichromate of potash.

This may require a further light papering and it should then be coated with white polish or A.C. lacquer (thin) which, when dry, may be lightly rubbed with fine steel wool and waxed.

Exterior woodwork. Western Red Cedar used for indoor cladding or panelling may be protected by the simple coatings indicated for limed oak and pickled pine. For exterior siding, however, this and other timbers need different treatment. The best preservative for exterior woodwork is paint where the pigments themselves provide an effective barrier in addition to the paint medium. Experience proves that if a clear finish is required then it is better to employ a penetrating, preservative liquid than to apply a surface coating.

A number of these penetrating fluids, incorporating paraffin, wax, fungicides, etc., are on the market. Some are obtainable in tinted form but the clear variety is probably the best since this allows frequent recoating without altering the colour.

Where old cladding contaminated by rain is to be treated it will be found advantageous to scrub well with sugar soap and allow to dry before treating with preservative fluid.

Garden furniture. The trick with traditional 'rustic' furniture is to play over the surfaces lightly with a blow torch. This has the dual effect of sealing the surface of the timber against the effects of the weather and of imparting a scorched or brown colour. The method is derived from the practice of charring the bottoms of posts implanted in the earth in order to prevent rot.

Modern garden furniture is often more sophisticated and made of teak and afrormosia. Two courses are open. Either the pieces are coated with three or four coats of a high quality exterior varnish (yacht varnish), or, at the other extreme, are treated with the penetrating liquids recommended for exterior woodwork. The varnished pieces will look cleaner and more 'finished' but will eventually require major retreatment. The alternative pieces will have a more natural appearance and will benefit from frequent re-treatment, but this treatment is very simple and inexpensive.

Painted furniture. The current vogue for painted furniture can be met very simply but not all simple procedures produce lasting results. It is wise, for instance, to be cautious with 'one coat' finishes. A more laborious procedure is likely to produce results which, while looking no better initially, will not chip and become shabby so quickly.

Old modern furniture should preferably be stripped clean and the usual precautions about washing-off observed. Then the painting can proceed after satisfactory surface preparation, filling of holes etc. (Fig. 75) in the orthodox manner. The filler should be cellulose, as used for cars. One coat of undercoating, papered down, and one finishing coat may be adequate. If more build is required then a second coat comprising half undercoat and half finishing coat may be applied before the final application.

Some of the modified paints incorporating polyurethanes and silicones dispense with undercoats. If these are used then intermediate flatting must be done with waterproof paper.

A superfine finish can be obtained with these materials if they are left for a month, again flatted with very fine abrasive and either burnished to a gloss finish or matted with fine steel wool and wax. This sort of sophisticated treatment is only suitable for articles such as chairs which have no large areas.

For new work a short cut is first to paint with an emulsion paint which will effectively obliterate and will dry quickly (do not thin the paint). The painting schedule may then be proceeded with in the normal way.

Fig. 75. Using a putty knife to fill a hole in a painted surface.

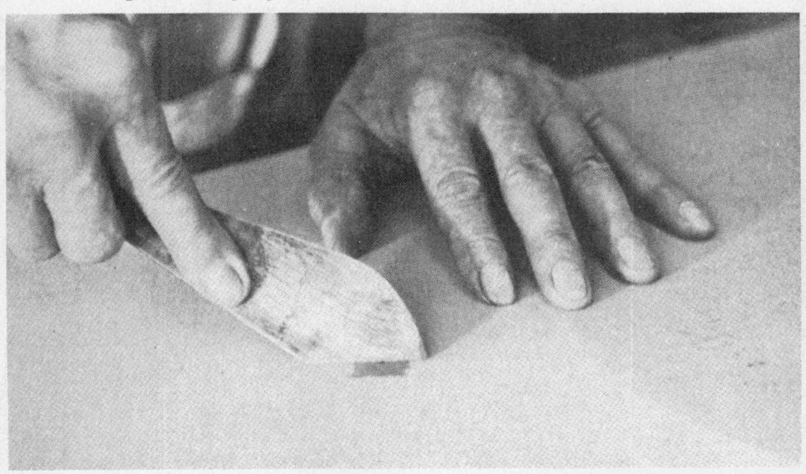

The picking out of carvings on Tudor work (or imitations thereof) is best done with the blues, reds, and golds of artists' oil colours. For the pastel blues and greens of the Adam period and some French furniture a keen colour sense will be required to mix the satin finish and undercoat not only for the right colour but for the right degree of sheen.

Metal finishes. Wrought iron may require stripping if it has been coated with bitumen paint or a crude job may simply be recoated with the same type of material. A black finish for iron is better achieved, however, by coating with a thinned dead matte black paint. Alternatively, thin a glossy black paint and stir in a proportion of gas black before applying.

For the gilding of metal the same procedures are adopted as for the gilding of wood. Aluminium paints are a good basis for other painting treatments if the surface of the metal is at all suspect (but do not be tempted to use such paint on a radiator or its effectiveness will be reduced by about 15%).

Small brass fittings should be stripped and cleaned before lacquering unless a used or 'antique' effect is to be retained. In the latter case they should simply be cleaned with detergent and relacquered when dry. They may then be brush dulled as required.

For the lacquering of small metal objects it is sometimes possible to dip them into the lacquer and after withdrawing them shake and turn them until residues have either been removed or have flowed into the main film. Special metal lacquers (not 'metallic') are available which are non-acidic and delay tarnishing. Failing these, a polyurethane lacquer, slightly thinned, will be found suitable.

Any new metal should be regarded as suspect until all traces of grease have been removed by washing with Varsol. Old metal should be examined for signs of corrosion. Loose corrosion particles should be removed with a wire brush and the surface treated with a rust preventative.

GLOSSARY

Most of the technical terms used in this book are explained in the text but other terms and formulations which may be unfamiliar are listed below:

Animal Glue Made from animal bones, fish offal and hides etc.

Applied Mouldings Decorative mouldings glued onto a surface, e.g. drawer fronts, doors.

Astragal A small plain semi-circular mould, often used on glazing bars.

Bevelled Sloping edge on a piece of timber, or metal as in the case of Bevel-edged chisel.

Blister Defect in a veneered surface, usually caused by perished glue under the surface.

Bracket Foot A type of corner foot often used on chests of drawers and heavy cabinets.

Brush-dulled Dulling a surface by imposing hair-line scratches in one direction by means of a brush fed with an abrasive powder.

Burnishing Polishing by means of friction. In some contexts (jewellery, metal) the term 'polishing' implies this only.

Carcase The main structure of a piece of furniture.

Caul A piece of wood used in the laying of veneer. It may be flat, or rounded if it is to be used for shaped work.

Cock-bead A small decorative bead which stands above the main surface of a drawer or door.

Countersunk To bevel the edge of a hole to allow a screw head to fit flush with the surface.

Clamping Pieces Pieces of wood used between the clamp and the surfaces of furniture being repaired to prevent damage. It is sometimes necessary to use shaped pieces to protect corners or enable a 'square' pull on the clamps to be obtained.

Cross-banding Border or band of veneer used as a decorative feature around the edges of a surface or top.

Decorative laminates Plastic sheets bonded together, and usually having a decorative melamine-covered surface, e.g. 'Formica'.

Dowel. A small rounded wooden 'pin' used for jointing. Usually made of Birch.

Draw-leaf A method used to extend the size of a dining table. The extending leaves are drawn out on guides from underneath the main top.

Drawer runner A small rail running from front to back in a carcase upon which the drawer slides. This is usually made of a hard wood.

Fall-Leaf A hinged leaf used on a gate-leg table.

Feather wedge A thin piece of wood or sawn-cut veneer, tapered across its width and used to repair surface splits.

Flush A term used when two surfaces are flat and level.

Gate-leg A hinged leg or gate used to support the hinged fall-leaf on a gate-leg table. The gate may be either single or double.

Glazing bar The framework used to support the glass in a glazed cabinet door.

Gut The main structure used to support glazing bars.

I.T.W. In-the-white, a phrase used to indicate that the wood or wooden object is unpolished.

Knuckle joint The movable wooden joint sometimes used on gate-leg tables.

Laminates Several layers of thin wood glued together.

Loose Tenon A method used to repair tenoned rails where it is not possible to 'spring' the framework, or where the original tenon may be broken.

Plugging The filling of old screw holes with wooden plugs, prior to refitting hinges etc.

Proud When the surface of one piece stands above the surface of another.

Rail The horizontal member of a framework or carcase, e.g. drawer rail.

Rubbed joint A glued joint where no extra support or clamping is used. The two surfaces are planed flat and level, warmed, glued, put together and rubber gently but firmly with the grain until adhesion is felt. The pieces must be left to stand until the glue is completely set.

Rubber tin An airtight tin in which polish rubbers are kept in good condition when not in use.

Rule joint A hinged joint, often used on gate-leg table tops.

Sawn cut A term used to describe the original method of cutting veneers.

Seasoning A treatment used on timber after felling and cutting to reduce its moisture content before it can be used for the making of furniture.

Shellac A spirit-soluble resin. The excreta of an insect indigenous to India and Burma. First collected for its red dye, used among other purposes for soldiers' uniforms — the famous 'thin red line'. Later development of aniline dyes made lac dye redundant. The resin then used for French polish and later for the early gramophone records. Still a valuable resin for a great variety of purposes.

Shrinkage A defect in timber due to unequal drying.

Splat Upright supporting pieces used in a chair back. Often shaped and decorative.

Storage life The length of time a product, e.g. glue powder may safely be kept.

Stub tenon A short tenon often used to join a drawer runner into a back of a drawer rail.

Striking Plate A small metal plate, often brass, used with locks and catches.

Stuck Moulding A moulding which has been worked into an edge, i.e. cut from the solid.

Veneer A thin layer of wood, originally sawn cut, now knife cut, used as a decorative covering on furniture surfaces. They are chosen especially for beauty of grain and colour.

INDEX

Printed in the United States